GROUND WORK

Robert Duncan

GROUND WORK

Before the War

A New Directions Book

Some of the poems in this collection first appeared in the following books and magazines: *Achilles' Song* (New York: The Phoenix Book Shop), *Beyond Poetry* (Australia), *Caesar's Gate* (Palma de Mallorca: The Diverse Press and Berkeley: Sand Dollar), *The Capilano Review* (North Vancouver, B. C.), *Credences, Dante* (Canton, N.Y.: The Institute of Further Studies), *Maps, New Directions in Prose and Poetry, Partisan Review, Paste Ups by Jess* (San Francisco: San Francisco Museum of Art), *Poetry, Poetry Review, Tribunals* (Los Angeles: Black Sparrow Press), *Wch Way*.

The following poems were originally published in pamphlets or as broadsides: "A Song from the Structures of Rime" (Malakoff, France: Chutes/Oranges Export Ltd.), "The Feast" *Passages 34* in *Modern American Poetry Conference* (London: The Polytechnic of Central London), "Bring It Up from the Dark" (Berkeley: Cody's Books), "Over There" (Storrs, Conn.: The University of Connecticut).

Manufactured in the United States of America
First published clothbound, in trade and limited editions, and as New Directions Paperbook 571 in 1984
Published simultaneously in Canada by George J. McLeod, Ltd., Toronto

Library of Congress Cataloging in Publication Data
Duncan, Robert Edward, 1919–
  Ground work.
  (A New Directions Book)
  I. Title.
PS3507.U629G7 1984   811'.54   84-4889
ISBN 0-8112-0895-8
ISBN 0-8112-0896-6 (pbk.)
ISBN 0-8112-0915-6 (ltd. ed.)

New Directions Books are published for James Laughlin
by New Directions Publishing Corporation,
80 Eighth Avenue, New York 10011

Contents

SOME NOTES ON NOTATION

Especially in the development of *Passages* I have workt with silences—with caesuras as definite parts of the articulation of the line, with turnings at the end of the verse, with intervals of silence in the measures between stanzas—related to phrasings and sequences of the whole. Silences themselves as phrases, units in the measure, charged with meaning. Significant pauses for the syncopation of suspense or arrest. In the notation of the text a line reading phrase-caesura-phrase-caesura-phrase would be considerd to be articulated into five elements. Note that more than one consideration may well be at work in a given verse.

The cadence of the verse, and, in turn, the interpenetration of cadences in sequence is, for me, related to the dance of my physical body. My hands keep time and know more than my brain does of measure. Stress patterns are dancing feet; my ear and voice follow a deeper rhythm, the coming and going of a life/death tide back of the beat of the heart and the breath. The literal time of the poem is experienced as given, even as the literal size of a painter's canvas is given. What is advanced in the process of the poem is the configuration of that given time. The counting of numbers, that numbers count in the structure, is an important aspect of the design.

The patterns realized are set; but the tempos go back to the body they come from in each reading. Three durations of silences are indicated by spaces of 1:2:3; which may be renderd 2:4:6 or 3:6:9—i.e. once the composition of the poem is there, the duration becomes flexible.

*

In the ground work there is a continuing beat that my body disposition finds and my moving hand directs I follow in reading. Its impulses are not schematic but rise, changing tempo as the body-dance changes. The caesura space becomes not just an articulation of phrasings but a phrase itself of silence. Space between stanzas becomes a stanza-verse of silence: in which the beat continues.

*

The space-period-space taken over from the later poetry of William Carlos Williams, at first un-defined, now means such a sounded silence, followd by the period in which the beat stops, and out of that cessation the beginning of the beat again.

*

Where lines of silence ("stanza breaks") come between pages, so that special notation is needed, the signs °° or °°° are entered at the top of the subsequent page to indicate the interval to be counted.

*

VERSIFICATION

The following are selected examples that I hope may cover the range of uses:

p.3 The opening line of "Achilles' Song" could be force-measured as an iambic pentameter, which may indeed appear and disappear in the courses of my cadences, for our poetic literature hammers away to imprint such regularities, as habitual to our minds as marches, two-steps, and waltzes. But the reader who seeks to render the line will mistake the verse or turning of the line. The voice is incantatory and its numbers are not the units of a metric rule but come and go in the poem: the count of syllables, or words, of phrases in the lines, of lines as present as potentialities of pattern as the sequences of vowels and consonants—but pattern is a local feature resonant to the formal field of the whole, and the poem has its formal identity not in itself but in the field of the poetry it belongs to.

*

All "typographical" features are notations for the performance of the reading. Margins signify. Thus, verse 2 of "Achilles' Song" returns to an inner margin, and in the linear sequence this is like the return of a wave to a systolic margin in the flux; in the "vertical" sequence of lines returning to the same margin an inner coding of the content emerges: "telling distant roar", "sounding and resounding", "into a moving wall", "been made in dread" etc. Unplannd, this is a set of cues. The returns to margins in the poem are not schematic but follow rhythmic and architectonic impulses in the felt flow of the on-going versification felt also throughout as a present structure.

*

The demarcation of stanzas then "counts": a space of one and a half lines counts as one verse of arrest or attention—a silence in which the preceding verse may be echoed and/or the following verse be awaited. But silence itself is sounded, a significant or meaningful absence, its semiotic value contributing to and derived from our apprehension of the field of the poem it belongs to.

*

Just as the cadenced verses have changing numbers, three beats or two beats—the rendering freely arising from the individual sense of the dance each time—so too the silences are cadenced.

*

p. 6 Verse turns to verse, reinstates itself.
Prose goes straight on to the end of its paragraph.

p. 11 There is a two-verse silence following the title,   and the line beginning "out of the sun" etc. picks up from the cadence establisht in the silence. (The concert master's hand may conduct the reading. On some recordings of my own renditions one can hear me mouthing the count in the silence.)

p. 13 If three beats are allowd for a single verse, the arrest after the work "stars'" will be nine beats. The intonation of "stars'" is the up-pitch of a suspended utterance, with "majesty thwarted" inheriting an initial stress.

*

p. 19 The section numbers need not be read aloud (though the names of the numbers frequently rime within the text). What is important is to hold the silences between sections as designating divisions, i.e. stopping and resuming the cadences.

*

CAESURAS

p. 3 Double space after a comma designates a caesura. On the following page (4) where, as in "Thetis, then," there is but a single space, there is no caesura.

*

p. 3 Where the verse turns on the pronoun "Her", as in line 2 "or I overheard Her", there is a demi-caesura, a hesitation (in which we hear "Her" as object turn into possessive adjective "Her roar").

*

p. 8 Caesuras here do not only punctuate the cadence but separate parts of the utterance from the vectors of their sentence direction so that their syntactic bond becomes suspended.

In *Passages* verses may be articulated into phrases or tesserae of utterances and silences leading to a series of possible sentences. As *Passages* themselves are but passages of a poem beyond that calls itself *Passages* and that is manifest only in the course of the books in which it appears, even so phrases have both their own meaning and yet belong to the unfolding revelation of a Sentence beyond the work.

San Francisco
February 1984

GROUND WORK

ACHILLES' SONG

I do not know more than the Sea tells me,
told me long ago, or I overheard Her
    telling distant roar upon the sands,
waves of meaning in the cradle of whose
    sounding and resounding power I
slept.

> *Manchild,* She sang

--or was it a storm uplifting the night
    into a moving wall in which
I was carried as if a mothering nest had
    been made in dread?

the wave of a life darker than my
    life before me sped, and I,
larger than I was, grown dark as
    the shoreless depth,
arose from myself, shaking the last
    light of the sun
from me.

> *Manchild,* She said,

Come back to the shores of what you are.
Come back to the crumbling shores.

> *All night*
the mothering tides in which your
    life first formd in the brooding
light have quencht the bloody
    splendors of the sun

and, under the triumphant processions
    of the moon, lay down
thunder upon thunder of an old
    longing, the beat

of whose repeated spell
    consumes you.

                        Thetis, then,
     my mother, has promised me
the mirage of a boat, a vehicle
     of water within the water,
and my soul would return from
     the trials of its human state,
from the long siege, from the
     struggling companions upon the plain,
from the burning towers and deeds
     of honor and dishonor,
the deeper unsatisfied war beneath
     and behind the declared war,
and the rubble of beautiful, patiently
     workt moonstones, agates, jades, obsidians,

turnd and returnd in the wash of
     the tides, the gleaming waste,
     the pathetic wonder,

words turnd in the phrases of song
     before our song   ...or are they

beautiful, patiently workt remembrances of those
     long gone from me,
returnd anew, ghostly in the light
     of the moon, old faces?

For Thetis, my mother, has promised
     me a boat,
a lover, an up-lifter of my spirit
     into the rage of my first element
rising, a princedom
     in the unreal, a share in Death.

     *

Time, time. It's time.

The business of Troy has long been done.

°°

Achilles in Leuke has come home.

And soon you too   will be alone.

--December 10, 1968

[NOTE: In our Anglo-American convention we would pronounce
the diphthong in *Leuke* to foreshadow the rime in the word
you--but in my hearing of the line, remembering the voice
of H.D.'s reading from her *Helen in Egypt,* the name *Leuke*
came to me sounded as in the German convention to echo the
diphthong in *Troy.*]

ANCIENT QUESTIONS

Are you brooding, Old Man, upon your works?
staring in gloomy depths where your deeds
incubate
Not with these seeds of discontent began
the curse that Earth's dark agents
sow in the dreams of Man.
Not with these cantos first we heard
where the ancient contest twixt
good and evil consequences ran.

And who has loosend the bonds of that snare?
Our spirits strive against whose toils?

In the first light after dawn, whose
boys, crying aloud to one another,
entangle the little birds in nets of
cunning Art?   Whose messengers
bring, already, news, alas, that
moves the heart against its will?
What instigator hid among these notes
painful harmonies in the song we sing?
What adversary brings our words to harry us,
ringing in our ears when we'd be still?

                    *

   Job, ʼ*Iyyôb*, deep rooted in enmity from long ago lasting he would
not know in himself against Him he obeys, cries out: *"Yahweh gave
and took away. Blessed be His Name in what He does."* He tore his
robe and shaved his head. The starry legions groand in his shame.

   You think I have but read this story? or that I have put aside
from my thought the despairing poet's face?   His eyes stare into
the shadows where the hostile flight of demonic wings shows and
vanishes, a flicker out of fire returning like rime the ominous
after-intentions of the Word shows Father to the thought. *"I alone
escaped to tell you,"* each messenger relates: *"The rest are dead
or dying. The walls of your story have fallen away."*

The name may be explain by the Arabic root `'wb`, I find--"*return,
repent*".   Rome in all its rimes remains, advances into ruin. And
the scholar tells us that before the name `'Iyyôb` there was another,
for in Bashan the prince of Ashtoreth, of Her with the lion's head,
Her of the roaring Sea, bore the name `'Ayyāb,` leading us far away
to the Akkadian cry `'Ayya-'abu(m)`--"*Where is (my) Father?*"

The Elohim brooding upon these Waters are appalld.

*

And you could recant, Old Man, recall?
Look deep into your sight and you will find
    a deeper blindness where you were stricken blind
--it is our own, revision of the Truth we see
    the Poet stumbles upon. Beauty
alone triumphant in the light of noon
    turns back Day upon itself
embitterd, and Night, bereft of dreams,
    is like a deserted railway station
after hours or in an age of inanition.

Will the last train never come? Come?
Or has the time of trains forever gone
    and left us?   Old...

And you do not think that Day and Night
    can speak?   Or that trains
were once the language of men's dreams?

He overhears their curses and embittering words.

The silence does not put my heart to rest
    but works me up, works me up.
A lonely signal in the night.
As if in Emptiness there were infant echoes
    crying, and Death
refuses me. Whom God has fenced about.

    Whose Way is hidden from him.

A SONG FROM THE STRUCTURES OF RIME RINGING
AS THE POET PAUL CELAN SINGS:

Something has wreckt the world I am in

I think I have wreckt
    the world I am in.
It is beautiful. From my wreckage
    this world   returns
to restore me, overcomes its identity in me.

Nothing has wreckt the world I am in.
    It is nothing
in the world that has
    workt this
wreckage of me   or my "world" I mean

the possibility of no thing so
    being there.

It is totally untranslatable.

Something is there that is it. Must
    be   nothing ultimately no
thing.   In the formula derived
    as I go
the something is   Nothing I know
obscured in the proposition of No-thingness.

    It is Nothing that has
wreckt the world I am in so that it is
    beautiful, Nothing in me

    being
beyond the world I am in
    something
in the world longs for

    nothing there.

DESPAIR IN BEING TEDIOUS

A long way back I look and find myself
as I was then I am, a circling man
in a seizure of talk that he hears too as he goes on.

The silence of the room was empty and I
cried aloud. At ten o'clock, went out
and walkt the empty streets again,

came into the crowded bar for company
and talkt of leaving when the rains began.
Some listend and some tired of me.

I do not know if I am bound
to run upon this wheel, wound up,
excited in a manic spiel of wheel in wheel,

or if I'm free to talk wherever they are free
to listen. A long way back I look,
and I was often disheartend there where I was.

Returning found the room deserted,
an empty space of Asia that crept into me.
I tried to die and did not. The hurt

was an empty place in meaning I turnd from.
That God was Asia I tried to say. Some were tired of it
and left, but there was too much that I had left to say.

I heard the drone of wonders as I went on,
a monotony of windings in the sun that led away
into a waiting in a room that Time itself be done.

What did I have to say? The talk was of Asia
and an emptiness in God that men have known
in deserts and in times like we are in.

What was I come to? As I come to,
your eyes have left me, and they stray

to find some exit from where we are.

"In Asia..."   There is a desolate possibility
I strive to get across. You gather up your things apart from me.
You do not follow, and I am lost therein.

There is in me a weary stretch I mean to say
some urgency that draws the matter out
I cannot come to, and I want company.

A long way back I look and find
I am still here. I hear the scraping of a chair,
excuses mutterd as they go.

The place is closing and I am alone I fear.
It's twelve to two.
I have come to myself. Good Night.

I will not need your help
me Lord. From here
Great Asia beyond the horizon of my sight

goes on to nowhere I cannot say
and in that continent as I go—
the hour stretches year on year.

THE CONCERT

Out of the sun and the dispersing stars
   go forth the elemental sparks,
   outpouring vitalities,
stir in the *Salitter* of the earth
   a *living* Spirit,
and the stars, mothers of light, remain,
   having each
its own "organic decorum, the complete
loyalty of a work of art to a shaping
   principle
         within itself"--

   that lonely spirit

having in its derivation likewise
the quality of the stars and yet

a severd *distinct* thing; and the stars also
   are and remain   severe and distinct,
     each being of the universe   free to itself
       having its own law.

Yet the quality of the stars
reigneth in the spirit; tho the spirit can
and may raise or drown itself
   in its own qualities, or take its life
in the influence of the stars, as it pleaseth.
   For it is free. It has got for its own
the qualities it has in itself, its own

   plot or myth, its feel
   of what   belongs to it

              --thus Boehme
in his *Aurora or Morning Redness in the*

oo

Rising of the Sun.

First there is the power, and in the power
    is the tone or tune,
so that all of creation moves with
    a music, the sound having its open
doors in the mind;   but in the heart
    lieth its fountain
            (as it doth also in Man).
    The second is *Mercurius*.   The musician

    has wound up his pegs
and tuned his strings.   He bends his head
    to hear the sound he makes
that leads his heart upward,

ascending to where the beat breaks
    into an all-but-unbearable whirling crown
of feet dancing, and now he sings or it is
    the light singing,   the voice
shaking, in the throes of the coming melody,
    resonances of meaning exceeding what we
understand, words freed from their origins,

    obedient to tongues (sparks) (burning)
speech-flames outreaching the heart's measure.

    It is the Star Betelgeuse, Alpha Orionis,
pouring its light within the depths,
        a single note its sphere,   each
"word" a severd distinct thing, Eternity
    already gone up into "MUST MUST MUST"
the Poet, his heart urgent,
    leaping beyond him, writes: "MOVE,
INSTANTER, ON ANOTHER!"   "Prophecy,

which uncovers the mystery of future events
but which also reveals what lurks in the heart
--prayers ... song and especially ecstatic

speaking in tongues"

They shout, leaping upon the tables,
   outpouring vitalities, stammering--

"Doubtless," the scholar remarks,
  "the content of such enthusiastic utterances,
   except where they are completely unintelligible,
   is always assumed to be appropriate,
but that is not what makes them *spiritual gifts*--"

   the isolated satyr each man is,
severd distinct thing, taking his word,
   his "mouth", his own, there, at the gate
or door   the sound forces in the mind
   from the heart-spring.

                        I saw

willingly the strain of my heart break
   and pour its blood thundering at the life-locks

to release   full   my man's share of the stars'

      majesty   thwarted.

John Adams, marginalia to Court de Gébelin's *Monde Primitif:*

"   We see not the End. We can foresee no end of the weakness,
"   Ignor[ance] and corruption of mankind"
                                                       then:
"   The beginning of the 19th century has been
"   de mauvais Augure"

    "ANCIENT REVERIES AND DECLAMATIONS
"   Fine
"   Fancies!   Preachers
"   of Order and public Felicity
"   are laudable and useful when they
"   understand themselves..."

"   The Age is not come.   The Order is not
"   arranged.

"   The reign of Saturn has not yet been born.

"   You must have lived many years after 1800 to celebrate
"   such Facts in your divine Numbers."

"   Something mysterious, however, under all this."

"   I call it spirit and I know what I mean as well as he does."

"   Americans!   Have a care   form no schemes of
"   universal empire.   The Lord will always
"   come down and defeat all such

                projects."

"Let the human Mind loose!   It must be loose!

            It will be loose!"

            Here one needs the name, the Spanish *Jesús*, or *Iacchus*

Iêsus. Say no more than the sound of the rime leads back
from the American cry *"Let the human Mind loose!"* to the
Jesús, Bridegroom of Saint John of the Cross, or to the
French /y/ of *Iacchus Iêsus* in Gerard de Nerval's ancient
theogony *"parée de noms et d'attributs nouveaux"*.

Your name, Jesus, has begun in my heart
again an allegiance to that Kingdom
"not of this World" but in the beginning of things
fallen apart.   There were a thousand seeds

and you were one. You were but one,
the one of a code or creed growing among us.
And the nine hundred and ninety nine
    divine persons of the Millenium, the sum of days and
    places
change places and times in your   being there,

take on the trouble as if time had a center
and spread out its story from Bethlehem.

20/12/69
        "For our sons still remember the burning of men,
    the burning, the shattering, the destruction
    of those days..."

Our sons will remember the loss of our rice in their bones
    deformd,
                "the loss of our maize ... fires over
    the whole province"
                    the loss of our rice.

    "The heavens were seald against us

    and leopards with burnisht skins
    came one by one out of the forest"
this: the Book of Chilam, the Jaguar Priest.

        The Four Directions

    must be let loose!   make it new!

                the human Mind loose!

"Alas for the joy of the living!

They must strip bark from trees for food,
and the claws of the lion's whelp draw blood
as they hide where we seek for food in the forest."

The Soul of the Great Stone wanders,   the old forest

takes over land once cleard,   deep

man finds himself outcast in his own nature

--*tanto è amara, che poco è più morte*--

the well of world-folk, the first people,
            source of our books,
becomes choked with sorrow,
      the depths of the sky raging...

  "Americans!"

                From the Land of Promises
      the blood of the Promised Land
      flows black   and a new Jesus
      jumps   under the blistering catafalque.

Xristus vincit   sees her in the King's mask,
Xristus regnat   seize her and be done with it,
Xristus imperat   raises a seizure in the heart of things!

  Two priesthoods are hidden in our hearts
  against the priests of this Christ and his

      Empire's hired murderers;   two
  hosts, messengers not of this World,
  remind us--

                Lords of Authority,
          Lords of Wonder--

two languages,   *deux fonctions*

            horoscopes et horloges,

one of the servants of the temple announcing
   the hour to the Goddess Herself,   then
the two ranks
   chanting in unison   in antiphony

       to the measure   the sistrum sounds

   the hour of day   the evening hour

   grief at His loss   joy in His finding

     the sistrum sounds,

                    they dance
for the hidden Isis,   for Life Herself,
   the sistrum

                 marking the measures
   death and resurrection of Osiris--

the old way thru the dark of the forest kept
               hidden,
                the old trails
   leading to ruins--

les deux autels à droite et à gauche
of which the second, the left, remain
   d'une conservation parfaite

--the text itself where I came to it
painted on stucco, Egypt, the image of
      Heaven, Africa--
Her land, Her plants, Her animals,
   Osiris,   the ever-flowing
returning river out of Africa, tears
   from the great Stone, the soul of the Day Itself
       wandering, at a loss, surrounded.

o o o

A gilded Venus, a Bacchus, numerous
    Hermes, the sum of days and holy places
having here Her precincts...

the sun going down toward Capri,
the moon slowly mounting in the smoke of Vesuvius   her face
        lightly veild,
ces deux astres qu'on avait longtemps
    adorés dans ce temple sous les noms
    d'Osiris et d'Isis...

Child of a century more skeptic than
    unbelieving, adrift
between two contrary educations,
that of the Revolution, which disowns
    everything,
and that of the Reaction,
which pretends to bring back the ensemble
    of Christian beliefs,

will I find myself traind to believe
    everything,

as our fathers, the scientists, have been

    traind to deny?

TRANSMISSIONS

[i]

ὄνομα βίος
ἔργον δὲ θάνατος

And in the whole community
the death of Man at work, bee hive
cells a-buzz with it,

the thriving of Death among us

the work of Art to set words

jiving   breaking into crises

in which a deathless strain moves thru

means without ends
Brancusi's towering column

moving into its true power,
into an imagined "endlessness", each stage of the form

dying upward, giving way

measures moving   in eternity   unmoving.

[ii]

"The color of my brother's keloid
mixes together with my feeling.

What I saw directly

that's what I remember..."

o o o

                    How he died

                    I live.

The color of his burns,
        the color of dried squid,   a tower

                the broild flesh

mixes together with my feeling,

gathers in the color of words a cry

        that stains,   moving upward.

                [iii]

        men's Good   "as naive and incoherent"

        as their Evil   "experienced and lucid"

                [iv]

    The "I" passing into sIght,

    the Mind   wherever
            it touches   blindly

forming this eye at the boundaries it knows,

    the brain's oracular stalk inciting
"that skin as though it knew and sympathized",

        dreaming of the Light to come,
    prepares the four-fold layers of Whose cup,

and from the World   Relays of electric disturbance run.

oo

Wine of color and dimension   where cells
"lay themselves down by becoming them themselves"

      transcending virtue
      transcending knowledge

        κρείττων ἢ ἀρετή καὶ
        κρείττων ἢ ἐπιστήμη

      transcending the Good Itself and the
        Beautiful Itself

        αὐτὸ τὸ ἀγαθὸν
        καὶ αὐτὸ τὸ καλόν

seeing so absolute is the skin
  a-swarm   eager to see

     "when set into motion and shaped and
     quickend by Mind, changes"

       the burnt color coming forward from Memory
           into the column of Being

"into the masterpiece, namely this World"

            --no one
    nor poet
    nor writer of words

can contrive to do justice to the beauty of that
  design he designs from.

      We pretend to speak.   The language is not ours
and we move upward beyond our powers into

    words again   beyond us   unsure measures

   the poetry of the cosmos
     τὸ κάλλος τῶν νοημάτων τῆς κοσμοποιίας

   transcending
   speech and hearing   λόγον καὶ ἀκοὴν   faltering.

"Under the graver's hand

oo

       the minutest seal   takes in
                  the contours of colossal figures"

   never abiding in the same state

   "For we must think of God as doing all things

      simultaneously"

                  [v]

     To unglue the up-tight esthetics
        undo your mind from the metric
              standards,   let space and time

surpass your uses--

      It must be made loose!

   Scriabin's *Third Symphony*
   König Ludwig the Second's
      Wagnerian daydreams and nightmares,
   Swine-burn's auto-eroticism then?   those
      compulsive urethral rimes,   the sound
      meant to keep the tympanum head
      restlessly throbbing?
   that Creeley and I agreed we could not
              read much of,
      having that injunction from Pound
      to direct into specifying energies
            the thrill of an other ways
            overpowering sensation

   --a Protestant dynamic!   the line

   a trial,   each element a crisis of attention
      yet--

      LET THE LINE SURPASS YOUR USES!   the command

oo

                comes into the works.

Not one   but many energies shape the field.

    It is a vortex.   It is a compost.

In brute strength and the refined alike
          the creative works

    by focus and diffusion, by potency

of the pure released form, the clean

        realized ovoid dream of Brancusi,
          Pythagoras made tactile,
or, at Tirgu-Jiu, the Column
    "which, if enlarged, would support the vault of Heaven"

          conceived to be Endless.

    The Cubist definitions

(1969) no longer "modern", or the "modern"
    surviving only as its period survives, where
          sentiment 1925 triumphs,
    l'art moderne of Corbusier, Léger,
      Mondrian (in his own mind
                    allied with surrealism)
    De Stijl in this room mixt with Gustav Moreau's
      deathly languishing heroes--Oedipus, Odysseus...

In the death-throes, scenes of the life
      dying come forward, foreword
to the texts of Hell and Heaven,   transient
      and transitional poems

    And

this art   an aggregate of intentions.

          And by corruption

(purity itself pent-up for corruption)

°°
over this gateway of a whole civilization

carved the words: *unless the grain die.*

A million reapers come to cut down
the leaves of grass we hoped to live by

except we give ourselves utterly over to the

end of things.

THE FEAST

     The butcher had prepared the leg of the lamb.

        "Its only mouth being spirit"   we prepared richly

      clothing its flavor in a coat of many colors.

 To 1/2 cup Dijon mustard

add 1 tbs Kikkoman soy
    1 tbs Pickapeppa sauce (Jamaica) made from tomatoes, onions, sugarcane, vinegar,
                                      mangoes, raisins, tamarinds

  mainly that it be dark and redolent of tamarind

--but the true measure is hidden in the fingers' feel for the taste of it--

  and garlic

  rosemary   ground in the mortar
  salt, pepper, and drops of oil   workt into the emulsion...

         We have come to the Festivities!

 The recipe appears
    between fond thought
    and devout actualities,   at this table

        we play the host,   the guests

gather round

    pleasures of the household,   the fine

       burnt smell of the meat   pleasing to the nostrils, yet

   this house is not Jahweh's --carrots, celery, onions, zucchini   cookt with yogurt
                          in the meat's company,

     for Cain's sacrifice in these devotions likewise

      satisfies.

The smith   the single most important craftsman

for the Bedouin   ritually impure   excluded from intermarriage and from
         eating in the company,

blacksmiths   a pariah caste   only the gods protect them,

    Cain, tribal father of the smith and the musician with his zither,
         patron of bards, founder of cities...

              Weavers, potters, and carpenters   appear to be foreigners to the tribe.

The Bethlehem Steel Company now in the place of the Moravian smithy at Bethlehem,

         this turmoil of peoples in the place where the City was!

    Milk of the mother, seed of the father, cream, barley and wheatgerm.

Carl Sauer in *Land and Life:* "We have neglected the natural history of man"

    "Institutions and outlooks have their origins in time and place;
         they spread from one group to another"

    "origins, derivations and survival   the basic determinations"

    "we know even the logos" --taking meaning and sound in our language as His
         attributes-- "only as a term in culture history"

                         in the Orphic rite
              the suckling lamb or kid

                         in the dream
         (though I was awake or my mind
              was wandering for a moment) it came

         in another spelling:

                    EVE is EWE

    in the cauldron of regenerations   fallen

         feeding on milk as though we were born again.

    On *this* side   Man's fortunate feast,
         harvests of his growing mastery   over his nature,

    "Antiphonal to this   the revenge of an outraged nature on man"

°°

The shit of the sheep does not redeem the shifting sands the script rock surfaces,
    wastes left after ancient over-grazing devourd landscapes

  "Lapse of time brought no repair"

                                    the dirty streams...

    The hosts have gone down to the edge of the sea,
        time has swept their tents away.
    The air we breathe grows dark with the debris of burning fats
        and dense with animal smoke.   All day

    exhausts pour forth into the slues of night their centuries.
        The black soil scums the putrid bay,

    the light is acrid to our eyes, and all the old runes
        thicken in our minds.

    Gē stinks to Heaven from the dumps of sleep.

    And where her children dream of Chaos come again,

        undoing the knots and twists of Man we roast the Lamb,

    flesh as we are flesh burgundy wine as our blood is wine,

            the red glow in the crystal the fire in the depth of her
      remembering

                hunger taking over the taste of things

                the sun's rays curdle in the pot

                        as in the first days
    the kid or lamb seethed in the mother's milk

    the thirst in the desert the hot meat

            ready in our need for it.

27

BEFORE THE JUDGMENT

> Discontent with that first draft.   Where one's own
>   hatred enters   Hell   gets out of hand.
>
> Again and again   Virgil   ever standing by Dante
>   must caution him.   In Malebolge
>
> where the deep violation begins,
>
> *Mentr' io laggiù fissamente mirava,*
> *lo duca mio, dicendo "Guarda, guarda"*

and here,   wrapt in the stench of vegetable rot,

> destroyd forests and fields,
>   and from the villages   the putrid dead,
> phantasms of industrial enterprise
>   swell fat upon the news of the daily body-count;
>
> after the age of lead, the age of gas, fossil fuels
>   oil slick on the water, petroleum spread,
>   the stink of gasoline in the murky air,
>   the smoking tankers crawl towards Asia--
>
> men with fossil minds, with oily tongues
>   "to lick the mirror of Narkissos",
>
>   oil slick over the pool there...
>
>
> where not only that first face saw but how many others
>   work in the industries of *this* Hell,
>
> betrayers of public trust --under Johnson,
>   monetary expansion   to finance the War
>   the modern form of "printing press" money--
>
> but their deals and names   sink into the mire,
>
> new faces and souls to work new damnations
>   rise to the surface
>
>   *quando il maestro mi disse "Or pur mira!*

che per poco è che teco non mi risso"

Dante being so drawn into a fascination by the controversies of the place

"And as one who dreams of something hurtful to him," he tells us--
    "and dreaming   wishes it were a dream
so that he longs for that which is, as if it were not"

Again his words come into ours and Virgil's words would draw me back

        into the orders of his art.

[Brought into English prose by John Aitkin Carlyle, 1849,
    revised in 1867, of whom his brother Thomas Carlyle wrote
"I wish him to be regarded as my second self, my surviving self"
--the text then belonging to the Mystery of these Passages--

for after Carlyle's *"The Hero as Poet: Dante, Shakespeare"*
Ezra Pound's *Spirit of Romance* opens our own period with his
announcement that *"The study of literature is hero-worship"*

            Poetry having also its liturgy]

For they go about everywhere over the earth,

    attendants, daimons not only of men but of earth's plenitudes,
    ancestral spirits of whatever good we know,

            wherever judgment is made   they gather round watching,
            what the heart secretly knows   they know,

clothed in mist, golden, ever existing, the host that comes in to conscience,

        deathless   they swarm in Memory and feed at the honeycomb.

    τοὶ μὲν δαίμονες ἁγνοὶ Hesiod tells us they are calld   these

        truly *full of awe* holy   unstaind by bloodshed

ἐπιχθόνιοι spirits of earth   καλέονται they are named.

        We call them by name.   The Master of Rime is among them.

And She   whose breast is in language   the Overwhelming

    sends her own priestesses of the Boundless to these councils of our boundaries,

    divine women of that generation, shores and islands their precincts.

And that there are islands in Time,

and even in War,   and in the Time of Retribution

(his Hell   our commonwealth)

they return to us,

ἔσθλοι   abounding,   Mind returning, a Child, to the Goods of the Intellect

as if to his Paradise, a secret state of Mind we obey,
shaking the powers of this state from within.

Each actual moment   a seed,

where Love enters   the Milk-Light flows from the Center.

The Golden Ones move in invisible realms,
wrapt round in our thought as in a mist,

and the forces of Speech give way to the Language beyond Speech,

the Sea the sea reminds us of,
the Hosts of the Word that attend our words,

even in the surge of recognition our own grasp faltering
we can barely read, we are unsure even of the meaning that haunts us,
--it is all Greek to us-- having what ground here?

unsteadily,

slowly, piecing out this passage of Hesiod that has long lingerd at the threshold of the poem,

evoking from the steady clear flame that drew us   its secret

and from the ancestors of the household we keep even in adversity

their voice   my voice   we come upon the fire   hidden, smouldering

we thought lost beyond reach...

Can you give me a light?

(He leans forward in the dark of yearning fearfully unprepared)

In the shed there is only a smoky lantern we work by.
    The cows stir in their stanchions.
        We kept the old rituals only one season.

And if you have ever kept my orders   I shall stand by you.

And Virgil to Dante: "Even now your thoughts have enterd into mine,
    with similar act and similar face; so that

    of both I have made one resolve."

So there was a covenant made with Good and into its orders I was born.
There was a covenant made that we call the Age of Gold, the Ancestral Design,
    and this alone governs what endures.

And I was immersed into the depths of the Water,
    let down by that man who stood for my Father
    into the Element before Intention

(or, in another version, cast into the Flood
    drownd in the rage of the Mother of What Is).

I am speaking now of the Dream in which America sleeps, the New World,
moaning, floundering, in three hundred years of invasions, our own history
    out of Europe and enslaved Africa.
Tears stream down to feed the Deeps below
from those eyes in which the spirits of America's yearning
come and go, broken, reassembling, enduring, defeated...

And will there be men to come who will remember
the names of the presidents, governors, mayors
    this profound Evil has placed over us,
each appropriate to his circle of the Inferno?

the powers of business and industry taking over government
    --War, the biggest business of all--
the interests of property the ultimate basis of this order?

They gave us the business. And Congress divided,
but the majority again and again for self-interest and profit
and to make good the Lie
    against the well-being of the people,

armies abroad and spies in every nation, false witnesses,

and at home the cops in the street now, "the law" supplanting the Law,
    having full mandate from the courts to kill without question,

back of the scene the bosses and war-mongers, misusers of the public trust,

        heads of the Hydra that Pound named *Usura,*

remember this time   for it returns   this betrayal of what we are

    among the people likewise   armd camps arise, and
            agents provocateurs keep the sources of trouble alive

        --in his Hell Cantos he named it

        "the slough of unamiable liars,
                bog of stupidities,
        malevolent stupidities, and stupidities"

            --we've got it   with new faces.

    In the highest   this hatred

doing away with public services as the cost of the government's self service rises,
    in every domain fighting to destroy the humanities,

        in the lowest   as if it streamd out from the governing centers

        destroyers of cities and orders

...their public faces, names... Rubin, Hayakawa, Alioto, Reagan, Nixon
        as we go upward the stupidity thickens,

        reflections in the oil slick multiplied.

        The Hydra prepares in every domain, even in the revolution,

                his offices.

        His clowns come forward to entertain us.

And will there be men who will remember

the Devil's legions had their votes, ward-workers, enthusiasts, willing
agents?   And there came the amateurs of Hell, the volunteer demons
    hungry for the look of fear their eyes would
feed upon, men devourd by hatred devouring hatred. And certain tribes
    shouting their own outrages against Man's nature

32

oo

in that place   at Malebolge

Alla man destra vidi nuova pieta,
nuovi tormenti e nuovi frustatori,

in every party   partisans of the torment.

Tyranny throws up from its populace a thousand
tyrant faces,   seethes and dies down,   would-be
administrators of the evil or challengers of the establishment
seeking their share of the Power that eats us.

Se le fazion che porti non son false...

But whose face is this face?   so many
having only Hell's loan of a face at interest--

he was but one of the many frogs croaking
from the desolate marsh,   seething,   collapsing,
that they call the Law,   figments of the media surrounding them.

Is *that* a name?   Alioto?   There are a million
Opportunity, without generation, spews forth like him
        to take over our cities.

This Slough extends thruout the Time of Man.

And from that wretchedness he leans forth,

        fearfully,   as ever,   yearning...

"*In this mirror,*" the Angel replies, "*our Councils darken.*"

The president turns in his sleep and into his stupidity seep the images of burning peoples.
The poet turns in his sleep,   the cries of the tortured and of those whose pain
    survives after the burning survive with him,   for continually
    he returns to early dreams of just retributions and reprisals inflicted for his injuries.
The soldier gloating over and blighted by the burning bodies of children, women and old men,
    turns in his sleep of Viet Nam or,
dreamless, inert, having done only his duty, hangs at the edge of such a conscience to sleep.
The protestant turns in his sleep, setting fire to hated images,
    entering a deeper war against the war. A deeper stupidity gathers.

The Golden Ones, the ancestors of our Good, cloak themselves in Sleep's depth,

oo

                    eternally watching.

As if from the depths of Hell, the sleepers seek rest in what they are,
so that again   the Wish of Death lifts them
                        and passes over them.
                                        This pain you take
        is the pain in which Truth turns like a key.

This Confession that struggles within you   and grows,
this *History of My True Country*   that you have come to acknowledge,
will not let you alone. And the Eternal Ones of the Dream
cast you forth from them.

                The Guardian moves as I am moved.

It is like a movement perceived in a stone.   Beyond my will,
unwilling,   I am moved.
                        The Jews use the name *Israel,*
you use the name *America* or the name *Man,*   as if for a chosen tribe
or nation or for one animal species   the Grand Design labord,
                or for the Orders of Life labord,

but the Golden Ones meet in the Solar Councils
and their alphabet is hidden in the evolution of chemical codes.

            In this place the airy spirit
            catching fire in its fall from flight
            has started a burning of conscience
            in the depths of earth and the primal waters,
            and all of Creation rises to meet him,

            as if to answer a call, as if to call   into Being,
            forth from a raging Absence, even among men,
            the Body of "Man" cries out   toward Him.

Children of Kronos, of the Dream beyond death,
    secret of a Life beyond our lives,

        having their perfection   as we have,

        their bodies a like grace, a music,   their minds a joy, abundant, foliate,   fanciful in its flowering,

come into these orders as they have ever come,   stand,
    as ever,   where they are acknowledged,

against the works of unworthy men, unfeeling judgments, and cruel deeds.

SANTA CRUZ PROPOSITIONS

I

[10PM-1AM, 13-14, October 1968]

Troubled surfer seeking the about-to-break line
of the wave in it to ride   toward revelation,
the tide that would have carried you draws back
    from the litterd margin,

and the depth of the sea you would have borne forward

is the depth of an impending failure   among us who
if we fall from the board, as we must,
    fall into the facts of the polluted stream.

Poetry!   Would *Poetry* have sustaind us?   It's lovely
    --and no more than a wave-- to have rise
    out of the debris, the stink and threat
--even to life-- of daily speech, the roar
    of the giants we begin from,
primordial Strife, blind Opposition,
    a current that sweeps all stagnant things up
    into a torrent of confidence   beyond thought.

Even as we are most "sent", and the Man
    most present, exultant in the giving ourselves over
    to the forces that consume our knowledge, whatever
    fact having no more boundary than
    water within water,   and for you then most

the *cold* of the sea, the withdrawal from pleasure,

        the curve of the poem

                withdraws its promise.

They are not *with* it! --you are not   with it!

The very   luminous where-with-all, the lure
    looms now   over all   Truth   collapsing.

o o o

Ancient knowledge of the sea, vastness of ignorance,
     silence in *that* origin,   waste and empty,
about the inroads   as you read,   the shores
     suck at the glorious sweep of the abyss in time you are pondering.

The voice carries us on to our just rewards,
     and leaves us.   How long ago we left
Old Mama Mammemory long lingering
     half in and half   out of it,
and yet we sing still to *Her*,   to the
          shadowy Big Presence of her,
to the Dumb Waitress coming up from below,
     staring at the empty lift,   facing
          an insolence that refuses to answer.
Yet we need her.   We don't need her.

     We will invent lungs and breathe in the
          fumes of the green magic.
Yet we want her.   We don't want her.

     The Muse consumes utterly, Woman of Water,
Woman of Sand into which all that reaches her
     all-but-exhausted of us   sinks,   leaving
the element of *Her*   undisturbd,   It makes
          no difference to her.

     It is to say we leave her,   we leave
everything for her.   The mind is not content but
     must build   even of discontent   histories,
          palaces, commands, grand
          impositions   --all for *HER!*

The great treasury of spiritual things is all for *Her!*

And under Her wingspread, fascinated,
     the boy plays with his building blocks
--sad, deep, absorbd, utter solitude-- as if
     the element that surrounds him *cared*.

What does it mean that the Earth labors to bring forth?
     Is there a Sea of Land even as of Water
          swollen with What Is To Be?

○ ○

He is sleep-working amongst his important things
and, waking, will be in agony.   The green wave
     of a mothering silence surrounds him.
It is not a *care*.   Her name is Listening, but
     what does she hear?
Even aroused, staring avidly,
   she keeps her own counsels and will not
      answer his need but   absorbs it.
   She leads toward his
     increase in it.

[15 October]

And he would move Time or our hearts'
   feel of Time?   Old Mummummymurmurur
turns in the applause of her surfs
   and takes us with her   inevitably
      away from the light, westward,
   into the undertow and night of our species.
There is no dream in which the high throne
   of the poet's personal Empire does not finally come
      to the dark shore of *Her* flood
and his word-power go out futilely
   to war with the insolent mob where
     her boundaries advance.

Grande Mer, Atlantique, first condition
   from which I came and all the
     generations of me came,

[16 October]

now you send me   out of your way--
   that's your way--   just
when I bring up before you at last
   my heart in my mouth
     I'm in your way,

[18 October]

and you are all shores and cliffs, and I
   come in upon you among the suitors,
     among the wild horses of the sea-foam,

sons of Okeanos, Lord of the Motherland's
    outer boundaries,   inconsistently surviving--

    the transformations of Who-I-Am,
as if incomplete,   inconsistently surviving

    in me.

[19 October]

            Ur-Father, Hairy Bull of the Waters
bellowing in Her, He the depth of Her sounding
    arousing out of Her dream of Chaos
eggs of those forms that await the coming of Man

--Worlds, Seas, Tides of the Sun and the Moon,
    Titanic Storms of Being   --Hells, then!
            (This First Water may have been Fire)
enormous predications of the Gods
    and, afterwards, Divine Powers --gods

    daimons, presences of living things,

    fountains, trees, great stones, hearth flames

            --Heaven.

He was our Language come in to the Mothertongue
awakening Images, fecundities.
    They were One, He/She
of the Great Mouth Chaos became in them,
    Chaos expiring in the Speech of the Winds.

There must have been a heart in that mouth, for,
    children of that Mother-Father, our hearts are in our mouths,

and, in the beginning, an other Larynx,
a vocal chord in the throat before Time,
from which the consonances and dissonances of lives vibrate.

                    II

[20 October]

Madame Defarge of the Central Committee

has the *motif* of a secret revenge.
She has withheld the benefit of her judgment
and knots in the thread of his life to enlarge his Fate   her *own*

[21 October]   plotted deprivations of his sight.   He strains,
                    even as we watch,
at the restrictions of his mind, wrestling
not with an angel but with a gnat he thinks she has
raised to challenge him.   It is the *Angel* "Gnat"
who stands at the Gate of the Claim he would make
      to the exalted rank he sees
accorded to the persons of Socrates and Kierkegaard,
      grand PhDs of an academic Immunity
               he does not see   as it is
shaken in the terrors Mind knows in Her thrall.

                    "Soccer Tease,"   she mutters
where he does not hear,
*"is my Saint, for he has drawn from the poisond deck
of youth's lure in his sight Alcibiades the Tyrant
the corrosive sublimate of a hindrance in Love;
and his face, that pug-satyr, leers up from the fumes
of drunken Sleep with an assumed knowingness about his
gnawing Nothing so that he wants Knot*
      that has befuddled Philosophy with method.
Him and his nosey sayauton!

[26 October]   *Diotima, my handmaiden--"*

Here began World War III against the Fathers.

      The four Knights of the Court in Mescaline

"showd him the picture-card of the Eros before Eros,
      the terrific first Mover at work toward Love"

found a conviction in him and commanded

   and I shall take both parts myself as well as I can:

Junked cars line the muddy road to the shed, and a chicken,
a rooster, a cat and a dog

   "What do you mean, Diotima, is Eros then evil and foul?"

°°
Frazier's residence was a dilapidated cowshed behind a half-
dozen larger similar structures

"He is a great demon, and, like all spirits, he is
intermediate"

"as brought to you by the people of the Free Universe"

"He the mediator who spans the chasm which divides them
--the divine and the mortal"

"Knight of Wands, Knight of Cups,
          Knight of Pentacles, Knight of Swords"

"and through Him the arts of the prophet and the priest"

The victims, their hands tied with scarves, were shot and
thrown into the pool of the $250,000 Ohta home, a half-mile
from Frazier's ramshackle cabin

"sacrifices and mysteries and charms, and all"

reachd by a flimsy swing bridge

"prophecy and incantation find their way. The wisdom
which understands this"

                              (Indefensible!)

Hidden under trees, however, are the camps of young people
with wild hair and outlandish customs

"went into the garden of Zeus and fell into a heavy sleep"

                         the older residents
resent, and increasingly fear.

"In the first place he is always poor, and anything but
tender and fair, as many imagine him. He is rough and
squalid .. on the bare earth exposed he lies under the
open heaven"

"materialism must die or mankind will stop"

"and like his mother he is always in distress"

"He really flipped out," said Michael Rugg, an artist who
lived near the shack occupied by the 24 year old Frazier,

a bearded highschool dropout and unemployed auto mechanic.
                    "VIOLENT EXPERIENCE"
"It was really a violent experience.   He wanted to sell
everything he owned. He wanted his wife to get rid of her
daughter and go with him into the woods. He wanted to do
extreme things."

> *"Like his father too, whom he also partly resembles, he
> is always plotting against the fair and the good;   he is
> bold*   (a bully!)   *a ruthless hunter"*

[11:30PM, 27 October]

Sheriff James said that many "frightened residents had been
calling the sheriff's office but..." "there was no real reason to believe"

> *"always weaving some intrigue or other, fertile in resource
> ...terrible as an enchanter, sorcerer, sophist"*

              "that any particular people you see are the
real suspects. Dr. Ohta himself had a gun which we have
recovered."

                         Every man armd!

         To keep the Peace!

   "and dead at another moment"   In Need!

frequented by tough motorcycle gangs and hippies, and hidden
at the end of a dead-end road in a canyon of the Santa Cruz
Mountains 15 miles from the city

> *"and again alive by reason of his father's nature.   The
> truth of the matter is this:"*

              Need. He was not careful, the wise man said,
of what he needed but, heavy with soma
     that drunkenness beyond care
              went into the sleep we call
the Garden of Zeus
                   to sleep in Sleep   where
        the Woman who begs at the Door of the Soul,
        Abject Poverty, crept to his side, whining,
        and lay with him.   Knowing nothing,

```
          what did he dream
      of cold that goes forever begging    as she invaded
          his rich nature,
      sharpening for her moment  his self satisfaction
      to cut the flesh of his side in sleep and
          aroused him    to conceive
```

"a severe personality change after taking the hallucinogenic drug
... a revelation!"

```
          Whạt does he desire?    What!

              Does he desire?
```

"misuses" he desires "the natural environment" he desires
"or destroys" he desires "suffer" --it is like a fire in him--
"the penalty of death" he desires "from this day forth"
he desires "comrades" he desires "death" --the fires of it
burn-- "against anything" he desires "not" he desires
"natural life" he desires "die" he desires   "stop"

```
[28 October]        Mankind must stop!

              She dances upon his heart!

    His Nature      tramples his heart!
```

[12:20 Midnight, 27 October]

*"There is Poetry, which as you know, is complex and manifold.
All creation or passage of non-being into being   is poetry or
making   still, you know, they are not poets but*

have other names"

The note, signed with the names of the four "court" cards, was
found under the windshield wiper of Dr. Ohta's maroon Rolls-
Royce that blocked one driveway to the hill top.
                    "WORST CRIME"

*"And the same holds of Love. But I say they are seeking
neither for the half of themselves nor for the whole"*

"the Free Universe" - "the natural environment" - "death
by the people of the Free Universe" - "I and my comrades
from this day" - "death for freedom" - "natural life on

this planet"

*"And they will cut off their own hands and feet and
cast them away. "*

They found Frazier asleep and took him into custody without
resistance.

He didn't resist   what moved him!

*"Do you not see how all animals, birds, as well as beasts,
are in agony*
concernd with music and meter?"

"World War III" on despoilers of the environment!

taking a .38 caliber pistol and knapsack of food he left
behind his wallet, driver's license and a book on Tarot

--it was the music of the Tarot that moved him--

"a perpetual loss and reparation
hair, flesh, bones, blood--

"She frowns and contracts and has a sense of pain"

Madame Defarge signals the Court that the Sentence is at hand.
Her secret *agents provocateurs* stir among the Listeners,
fingering the men who are to die

"in order to give birth"   a new Law and Order!   Anew!

III

[7:30AM, 28 October]

But it is Denise I am thinking of--

"I feel terribly out of touch with you and fear
you may be hurt at my silence but I just can't
help it."

In the depths of the woman

in love,   into friendship,   the old injuries

out of Love,

oo

out of the depths of the Woman's love,

SHE appears, Kālī dancing, whirling her necklace of skulls,
trampling the despoiling armies and the exploiters of natural resources
under her feet.   Revolution or Death!
Wine!   The wine of men's blood in the vat
of the Woman's anger, whirling,
the crackling-- is it of bones?   castanets?
tommyguns?   fire raging in the ghettos?   What
is the wrath of Jehovah to this   almost blissful Mother-Righteousness
aroused by the crimes of Presidents?

"And I know such violent revolution has ached my marrow-bones,

> *my soul changing its cells"*

--so immediately the lines of her poem come into mine.

                        She changes.

Violently.   It is her time.   I never saw that dress before.

I never saw that face before.

   ["When she is in the depths of her black silence," he told me,
    "Phone right away. Don't think you know what to do to help her.
    She is dangerous."]

Madame Outrage of the Central Committee
forms a storm cloud around her where she is brooding. This Night
opens into depth   without end in my life to come.

   The Four Winds come into the Womb of Her Grievance.

            Every woman   an Other   I fear for her.

She has put on her dress of murderous red.
She has put on her mini-skirt and the trampling begins.
She has put on her make-up of the Mother of Hell,
     the blue lips of Kore, the glowering
     pale of the flower that is black to us.
She has put on her fashion of burning.

Her tenderness grows tender, enflames,

and, from the painful swelling of that history to come,

"My cracked heart tolling such songs of unknown morning-star ecstatic anguish

...   unquenched desire's radiant decibels"

I too know in her telling and

At the storm center
her flashing eyes,   a shouting
in the street rises and against

the doctrine of Love as Need that Plato's Socrates tells us Diotima laid on him,
that untrustworthy Mind's father turning the Mother's words to suit his purpose,
against the pleading croon of the folk-rock singer
to put down the rage of revolt with *Love, Sweet Love,*   she cries

from the center of terror
that is the still eye of the storm in her:

"There comes a time when only Anger is Love."

A GLIMPSE

        Come, yellow broom
and lavender in bloom,
the path runs down to the shady stream,

and yet by your magic and the loud bees'
        hum,
        perfume of sage and lavender in bloom,

hot and dreaming in the morning sun,
I ever from where I am return,
as if from this boyhood privacy
my life burnd on in a smoke of me,

mixt with sage in the summer air
        and lavender,
and the stream from its shade
runs down to the bay and beyond to the sea.

AND IF HE HAD BEEN WRONG FOR ME

yet he was there, and all my thirst
gatherd in the thought of him that year,
a tall liquid presence of the man,
a river running in the sound of him,

sun dazzle in the shallows, shadows
in the pool beneath the rocks.

It is a place of early lonely thought,
impatient revery of a cool green.

It is a glass of water
ever just pourd for me, a memory
kept silent come to speak.

FOR ME TOO, I, LONG AGO SHIPPING OUT WITH THE CANTOS,

my soul aroused to go forth on the godly sea, Pound then heroic,
setting keel to breakers, *our* keel,
the roar of surfs upon alien shores our boundaries--

And they, shifting, chimerical, raising maps of a poetry in my mind,
for me too, now, among the voices the ear finds, overheard in the blur,
    the cross-currents of the sea sound,
the continual murmuring and telling of their life times,
    small talk and great sentences, rumors of divine
orders and powers rising into
    shadows and radiance I not my eyes

see, for it appears to me or nearby might appear to me She
    walks upon the path the moon

spreads out upon the surface of the sea.

AND HELL IS THE REALM OF GOD'S SELF-LOATHING

"It burns me up to see the way He thrives in cheating"

    looks into what mirror
        to see

    what burning face

          in error

    I had thought my own
      what I could own.

Through all the torture overtaking me in passing,

    another flower, not of evil,

      shone.

CHILDHOOD'S RETREAT

It's in the perilous boughs of the tree
out of blue sky   the wind
sings loudest surrounding me.

And solitude, a wild solitude
's reveald, fearfully, high I'd climb
into the shaking uncertainties,

part out of longing, part   daring my self,
part to see that
widening of the world, part

to find my own, my secret
hiding sense and place, where from afar
all voices and scenes come back

--the barking of a dog, autumnal burnings,
far calls, close calls-- the boy I was
calls out to me
here the man where I am "Look!

I've been where you

most fear to be."

FRAGMENTS OF AN ALBIGENSIAN RIME

Abel was a butcher.
He dealt in blood and meat.
He burnd the bloody carcass
and the sacrifice was sweet.

And Cain he was a baker.
He brought cakes and ale.
Or was it the Bread, the ripend Wheat-Head,
And a grail of red red wine?

The Father threw his offering down
and trampled on the Vine.

        *

Who was the Fiend upon the road
Who twisted Jacob's thigh?
And was it Truth he struggled with
Who named him Israel,
setting his kin
apart   from other men?

        *

He hung His Son upon the Butcher's hook.

At Béziers, at Carcassonne,
the meat hung high,
the blood ran down.

O!

The constellation glitters.   Stars abound.
In every house   the night's aglow.   The window

     ...

Is   Χαω *Cow?*   !

     Compounded   Earth   Milk Maker
     the sweet myth mounting
          stems
          that from the understuff grow

in conversations with the light
     life's laboratories

          Gap

first large language into leaf

     I
          ever

     green

          horn   play

     my music

as it goes

          it comes to me.

     The tip

of the tongue

     before the mouth sings,

     in labor

°°
the world cow's lips
      from which

--What an opening of the night it is!--
      this window

      her dewy calf
  from his confinement
      the poem from the heart in labor

      springs.

BRING IT UP FROM THE DARK

Bring up from the dark water.
It will be news from behind the horizon.
Refugees, nameless people. Who are they?
What is happening?   I do not know.
Out there.   Where we can see nothing.
Where we can do nothing. Men of our own country
send deadly messengers we would not send.
The cold wind of their desolation chills the first hint of morning,
rumors of burnd houses, smoking fields, and now wraiths
of the dead men daily they kill rise
against us.   It will go against us,
    pass, sweep on and beyond us.

The great house of our humanity
no longer stands.   Men from our own country
stamp out, burn back, flush up from their refuge
with gasses, howling or silent, whatever
human or animal remains living there.

Bereft, the mothering sky
searches our faces, searches my heart.
What have I to do with these things
that now I am left destitute.
In the midst of my happiness, the worm
of man's misery coils in my heart.

Dream disclosed to me, I too am Ishmael.

STRUCTURE OF RIME XXVII

   The shadow of the Muse falls across letters of the word that rises
now I see from his work, and, obedient to her command, my mind goes over
to his.   Into my pupils returns a studying rapture.   From these hiero-
glyphics the sound arose.   Abraham in Egyptian depths of America dreams.

My companion, the artist of the picture-book I shall ever return to,
meets me there.   *"She has commanded the opening of the Interior Palace,"*
he says: *"All the figures of the Made World return with you to undo What
Is She loves."*   Into the shadow jewels formd in the glances of terrible
men shine.   And, from the ruind sockets of other civilizations eyes from
animal and child faces burnd back into sections of our own world from
the suffering skull pull at the chords that we have never severd.

In the Hive of Continual Images the Bees, angelic swarm, build in the
visible cells a language in which they dance.   The honey runs down from
the beasts workt in the walls of the cave, from the divine figures, the
negro kings under the crowns of the two kingdoms.   Underground, the
terrors and judgments.   *"The guard there,"* my companion that came to me
as he was sent tells me, *"opend and closed the leaves of Bosch and all
the trees of my soul opend and closed to see the fires that burnd in the
Day he saw.   So, I have assembled all the things and beings of my world
to read them."*

   The honey runs down from the emblematic banners, the faces of Fate in
the tarot suite, the alchemical allegories, golden and black.   Deranging
the intention of Dick Tracy to track a diracy rat he saw there, the inner drama of a violated identity shows its face.   In the work the Muse
commands, the poet of the visible dissembles and reassembles depths and
faces in Persephone's pomegranate.   In every red seed a life is planted.
And all the scenes and deeds in which Man has illustrated his nature--the
grievous and the stupid with the joyous and the brave to know the heart
of things, the households and furnitures, the sacred groves and gardens,
the battlefields, corpses, empires--grow again.   Dancing in the single
cells of the geometry in which they are planted, the bees of heaven articulate in Its changes the Way the ephemeral blooms where the honey of
the Eternal again rises.

This has always been the One Art--the revelation, the moving picture, the

urgent speaking to us of the world we see that moved us to make even of
the sounds of our mouths an answering speech, the informing dance of
images into which the Eye opens. She sends Her bears to claw the archi-
tectures loose from perfection. The Opening of the Way again, the Wound
in God's side. Angry, confused, then a cloud in which the Queen is hidden, the workers are released from the old order into the Great Work
beyond their understanding. They must go beyond the bounds of their art.

But the new sweetness! The new ground of jokes and sadness! Anew,
the deadly stings of truth! Anew, the visible World speaks in passing
sentences of final things seen.

"Then, bury deep into the Visible," She commands us.   *"Return your
intelligence into the threshold of the real from the chamberd brain to
the seeing fingers of the eye that feels, to the equilibrations of the
inner ear to dwell in the light and dark of the rainbow from which color
streams toward the music sound imitates; in the heavy and light in which
desire arrives, burrow deep if you would reach that Grand Burial of the
Mind where it may rest."* In the dawn of the new artist's vision, the Old
World, let loose from what we thought we knew or would take for granted,
exhibits itself without rest.

STRUCTURE OF RIME XXVIII

IN MEMORIAM WALLACE STEVENS

  "That God is colouring Newton doth shew"--William Blake

    Erecting beyond the boundaries of all government his grand Station
and Customs, I find what I have made there a Gate, a staking out of
his art in Inconsequence. I have in mind a poetry that will frame the
willingness of the heart and deliver it over to the arrest of Time, a
sentence as if there could stand some solidity most spacial in its
intent against the drifts and appearances that arise and fall away in
time from the crude events of physical space. The Mind alone holds
the consequence of the erection to be true, so that Desire and Imagination usurp the place of the Invisible Throne.

    It is an angel then, weeping and yet ever attending the betrayal
of the Word I mean to come to in the end. For my sake, the blood must
be somewhere in time and in its own naming of place actual, and death
must be as my own awaits me immediate to undo from its reality the
physical body, all there is of the matter of me that is mine from me.
The would-be dialecticians--Inquisitors of the New Dispensation in
Poetry and Historians of Opprobrium, the Realists and Materialists--
come forward to hold the party line against his ideality. There are
too many listeners. There are too many voices in the one line. They
must enter the Ideal to do so, for he has changed his mind, as if the
Eternal existed only momentarily and went out with him. The Chairman
of the Politbureau gets his number and moves to isolate his heresy.
The number is no longer the same. He has gone back into the exchange
of numbers. The phone continues ringing in the pattern of the message
they strive to listen to report to the Bureau of Poetic Numbers and
Approved Measures.

    This is to say to the month of April and the rainbow dancer, I am
with you. I belong to the company without number. I shall live one
hundred years and then be gone. Here and now only I from this life
can come forward to impersonate the necessity of his being here. His,
the horizon. His, the perspectives and outlines. His, the regulation
of the relevant. I will willingly assume his numbers among my own.

    The rest is all Asia, the astral miasma, the Undoing we came from,
my version of Who-He-Is-In-Reality, the domain of colouring invading
the Responsible.

OVER THERE

                    where *thou* art

over here   where you are

                              not

I write   under this surd
   what is not   raised to its own power
Truth somehow   how
        I know not   agnostic
ultimately   you are
                              there
for me.

        Back of those words I read
you are not facing me.   A yearning,
a broken bridge from here to need beyond me
reaches,   and now
to impersonate one over there   every
one comes in.   Come in, Love.
Come in, Pearly Cloud.   Hairy, I read you
OUT. Come in.   I address you all
ways   as ever   In one

imagination   there is a bond   secret to my understanding   that fate the
structure of rime imitates commands.   Beyond my *Medieval Scenes* you went
to distil from the sensual ripening the poisons of an alcohol whose fumes
have toucht poetry with rages and hallucinations I but refer to you ate.
At the bile of Narcissus you croucht to rework his mirror as if to prove
a window or renew the useable surface.   Words come to.   The unuseable
surface.   The unusual, usual.   An age when hallucinations and rage are
in.   You reacht the works of Poetry ahead of us.   A head of ours in which
cross circuits of whatever we were I was not   you secreted there.   There
is an attractive distraction come in to the works.   Tik-tok reassembled
because of the genitals.   *"Hell-lo lit-tell gurr-El,"* it says to the
boy, *"I Met-a-tron."*   What is a tron?   *"In-viz-sib-bel hell-purrs,"* it
answers. *"Come in. Your well come. Your whirr-rrk well done. I like
it. Well done."*

All the water of our world come into a bed as insatiable as Los Angeles.
Oil of Life wells pumping day into night.   You master the surface of the

wasted waters to see a new face there. A nark's kisses. Seepage in the
dead pan underlying the painful grimace.

At heart you were bleeding and I refused the blood.   I turnd back from
the blood and withheld the cup. I withheld the question. I took back my
word from the bond I found terrible. The word of the bond remains bleeding. In the mirror next time I will wear a face that is black and trample
you out. In the heart of the new poetry you are hiding.   Away from me.
In the halls of air interim away from you I have created out of all the
old poetry left over I am. Over and out. Signd again. Resignd.   Tired
again. Retired. I opend a window in the wall of the old stuff and named
the bird I always hear singing a nightingale. It was the Larke, the
herauld of the Morne. No Nightingale. Night's Candles are burnt out.
The Night is over

there   where *thou* art   here   the Day .

THE MUSEUM

Grand architecture that the Muses command! my heart and breathing lungs mount the ascending tones in which your pillars swell, sound, and soar, above the struggling mind.   In the treasure room enclosed in sound, Muse upon Muse turns to gaze into the radiant space in building.

In certain designs they are most present, and in their presence I come, I realize, into their design. What I see now is a shadowd space, a shell in time, a silent alcove in thunder, in which the stony everlasting gaze looses itself in my coming into its plan.   It is an horizon coming in from what we cannot see to sound in sight that is female. Moving toward an orison of the visible. From this carving out of thought of an arrival, the figure of a womanly grace invades the sound of the heart that beats for her, and, in number, repeats in a run of alcoves --shadowd radiance upon shadowd radiance--beyond the body of this Woman, the body of these women. In the Museum--as in the labyrinth at Knossos, the Minotaur; as in the head of the Great God, the hawk Horus returning-- a Woman that is a company of women moves.

She will not devour the heart but holds it high in her command.   The shadow she stands in is the shadowing of the heart's ease. Yet now in an exaltation of this chamber my mind comes upon the Bestial Muse, the devouring *Impératrice* at the heart of the Museum. In the inner chambers of the heart of the building, the fountains of blood are all there is. And the laboring pumps that she hides there. And the locks and releases hidden there.

I am entirely hers in that confessional. Entirely shadowd. Entirely gazing. A route of seeing carved in stone. A stream of utter weeping in that stone suspended. And if I were a woman out of the man I am, a Poetess would burst into her lament and memorial for the man destroyd in her.

O Muses, ancient and overwhelming sisters we have so long playd in whose orders,
    you stand between us and our Father;
you lead us on into this vale between slopes flowery and sweet where
    all our grievances and memories of love run into song;

you come to meet us at the well you command in the midst of our thirst;
you hold us in the suspension of your regard,
and the smile of an appreciation we cannot fathom breaks away from us.

In the halls of the Museum, all that we meant to remember
—our passionate resolve, our crying out and our murmurous sigh—
falls into that fame that silences what we were. Was it for this
fame then that we cried out? Was it against this fame that we
protested? O Muses, aweful and brilliant in your drawing us toward
that grace in which the spine is curved into life to sound its
depth in fame, your fame catches my tears in its resounding
cistern. And every mammal weeping I hear, drip upon drip, as if
alone, resounding there. And birds and reptiles weeping. Cell
upon cell, in each, this shadow. In each, this Muse of a commanding
Art. In each, this falling into Time, drop by drop. In each this
eternal gaze. In each, this ultimate Woman. In each, this guile
without guile—the artful suggestion glancing, the terrible amusement, the call to grace that is drawn to dance upon hurt once more.

Now, deep, deep down in the underground of restraint, the
bass intoning of a Man begins, wonderous in its progression Male,
its thunderous resolve of a commanding sorrow. It is the Man that
men and women have dreamt deep in themselves to be their species
—for I came from the body of Woman into the thought of Man—and,
all of darkness, that Man in the light of Being groans and turns
upon Himself. A challenging tone that begins and passes into the
arrest of challenge. O mighty Worm that in the Cocoon of What is
slumbers! as you turn and intone your turning, the great women
in the Hall of the Muses appear to be statues groaning. The
poets whimper in their sheltering shadows, and, from their altars,
poetesses advance to sing once more as Sappho sang from the lyric
strain that Love that breaks us from what we are:

> ...irresistible force, bitter, sweet, that even now
> strikes us down, you have awakend what we feard we were, and,
> men and women, we are lost in you.   Pain
>
>   enters Being
>
>   drop
>
>   by drop.

o o o o

The earth in its deep foundations shakes
and tears the bindings of ancient buildings loose.

The Muses appear to be now
deserted cisterns in a row.

Was there in the beginning
    some vow I made
that has come due?   I know
    no more of Art than this--

a kind of play that when I was a child
    was fearful in its promise and yet
led from fear into a radiance, a brother's
    turning for a sister's kiss.

The Muses fade into dim images.
The images fade as if I made them up
and came out of making into a loss of confidence.

And now...   *Now . Now. Now .*   the poem sounds its refrain in Time

...there cometh as if it were an ancient return to rime,
behind and beneath the man I am, the sounding of an other, Man I am--
    Man!
in me. Alone. His ultimate aloneness
invading me. Invading my own utter aloneness in my time.
His promise, the promise of what Man is in me,
    reaches up and takes
into itself as a persisting need
    that dimness of the other side.

And Him *the gathering of shadowy Muses shakes.*

    It is the architecture then of arts inspired by confidences
of an earthquake yet to come. The Muses are of stone to be riven
from stone. And they dream--it is the vision of this very art in
which, out of no confidence, their confidential song comes into me--

    into the abyss they gaze   into which the Museum falls.

INTERRUPTED FORMS

Long slumbering, often coming forward,
haunting the house I am the house I live in
resembles so, does he recall me or I
recall him?   Seeing you the other day
long I lookt to see your face his, longing
without reason. I meant to tell
or spell your name, to dwell in the charm
I almost felt in the stone, the impassive
weight of old feeling, the cold awakening
I meant to tell you of, as if telling could reach you,
at last come into your embrace again, my arms
hold you, mounting, coming into your life
my life and interruption of all long lasting
        inertia in feeling,
arousal.
                In dreams
insubstantially you have come before my eyes'
expectations, and, even in waking,
taking over the field of sight fleetingly
stronger than what my eyes see,
the thought of you thought has eyes to see
has eyes to meet your answering eyes
thought raises. I am speaking of a ghost   .
the heart is glad to have return, of a room
I have often been lonely in, of a desertion
that remains even where I am most cherisht
and surrounded by Love's company, of a form,
wholly fulfilling the course of my life, interrupted,
of a cold in the full warmth of the sunlight
that seeks to come in close to your heart
                for warmth.

PREFACE to the Suite

     1

Childhood, boyhood, young manhood
ached at the heart with it, the unnameable,
the incompletion of desires, and at the margins
shook. O Wind, South Wind, dark
and laden with long awaited rains,
in me a likeness that is yours sings
--always sang--and now that manhood has grown full
and half a century of the seasons rehearsed,
again, again, adolescent to what new man,
you come in dreams and to the margins of my thought
stray.

       O Need, beloved Adversary to Love's settlements,
Invader, the halcyon days are over.
A violent season tears the depth of the blue.
The kingfisher turns from his studies where
his nature grows disquiet in him, some
wildness of a winter is all his, and
looks out upon the alterd scene it belongs to,
hunting.
        Today belongs to you, to the music
about to be heard, the distant luring call recalld,
the strain, the estrangement from all I knew,
another knowledge straining to be free.

O deepest Unrest, indelibly engraved in me,
the wilderness beyond the edge of town, the riverbottom road,
the lingering, the wandering, the going astray,
to find some wanton promise the derelict landscape most portrayd in me,
the fog's sad density of cold,
in me, the solitary and deserted paths,
in me, the marshy wastes, the levee road
where day after day as if driven by the wind
I impatient strode, day driven after day,
until the rush of impending weather was most me

in me, the dumb about-to-be, the country way
incapable of speech driven toward impending speech.

I was never there. He was never there.
In some clearing before I reacht it
or after I was gone, some *he*
had laid him down to sleep where Pan
under his winter sun had roused the wildness with his song,
and, long lingering,
the air was heavy with his absence there--
Lord of the Heat of Noon still palpable
where late shadows chill the dreaming land.

2

Ghosts and lovers of my sixteenth year, old themes
and changing keys of a persisting music,
here, the colors fade, I cannot recall the face, there,
some pattern revivifies the scheme. What
was the accurate contour of the fathering dream?

The year my father died died into me and dyed
anew the green of green, the gold gold shone from,
the blue that colors seas and skies to speak
of sadness innocence most knew, and into Man
a mystery to take the place of fatherhood he grew
in me, a ghostly bridegroom fathering his bride in me,
an emptiness in which an absence I call *You*
was present, a pride, a bright unanswering bliss,
consumed my heart. It was a fiery ghost,
a burning substitution darkening all the sexual ways,
striving in those urgencies to speak, to speak,
to heal unutterable injuries. It was a wounded mouth,
a stricken thing unable to release its word,
a panic spring no youthful coming could exhaust in me.

THE MOLY *SUITE*

NEAR CIRCE'S HOUSE

Not far from Circe's house I met a man,
derelict, swept by the winds, to whom I was
I knew an apparition of some plan
half-forming in his mind he and I were
as if driven to by assembling Fates,
and, "Where are you going?" I askt,
"You are so alone my own life
which was eternal and self-contain
opens up vast breaches of promise in the
thought of you you know nothing of."

Behind me as I speak to you I hear
all your men, your shipmates,
fallen where they are into evil ways, ensnared,
closed round in Circe's circles,
grunting, rooting, snuffling, fucking
at the gates. And in your eyes
I seek to open a gate that I would enter
momentarily.   I am trying to tell you
--Take my heart from me
and it will beat for you, wildly.

I am trying to tell you
Hermes I would be for you as I
have been for others to protect
in falling in love, take heart from me,
for from the very loom where She
weaves and undoes each night your odyssey
I bring this herb, black at the root
and milky white where it blooms.   See,

from the very ground here where we stand
I pull the magic plant that was meant
to help you enter and pass through
Her darkening intent.   It is the heart
I spoke of fed this stem in me,

torn out of its own darkness,
this herb calld *Moly* by the gods.

RITES OF PASSAGE: I

These are
the passages of thought
from the light air
into the heavy flesh
until from the burning
all the slumb'ring dark
matter comes alight,
the foot that has
its reason in bright ratios
it would measure

hardens and beats
the trembling earth,
reaches out of measure
into the hoof that
tramples
pleasure and pain compounded
into a further brightness.

Dark Satyr,
your blood is like a
light behind an
almond bough, now
something is taking
place in me
all nature awaits
behind the trembling
tapestry of leaves
and buds, of
hidden, about-to-be-
awakend birds.

The damp submissive grass

now stirs from sleep,
now turns in every
green blade grown
alert
with listening.

What is Spring
that everywhere bursts upon my world
with such a chorus of first voices
and to my flaring nostrils brings
rank odors of the root of things
but this--the year's like expectancy?

And half a century grows fresh in me.
A hearing stiffens, strains at the leash of a wild dancing.
As if answering an as-yet-unspoken need,
upon the brow of a silence behind my words
the pensive horns of a new yearning thrust.
The force of a rime impending runs abroad
forebodings at the edge we are in ourselves,

edge now of arriving hooves we
    almost hear, the prancing
advances in our feet,

edge now of the rush that attends
    your coming, where we are not,
an edge of home in me, of Pan.

MOLY

It is said that there in Her house you
    are not fair but,
cowering or covering, go down
into the beast's way, such is
    the sorcery of Her song.

The voice we raise in poetry

so that it seems lovely to be enthralld
    by words and truth
to be in soaring numbers and in rimes
    thickens and
goes down into the throat,
gagging, rooting in the grass,
    fertilities of sound,

snuffling, snorting, snared in a
delirium of snout and watering mouth
    incapable of speech,
all animal tongue and panting breath, the lungs
    sucking the psychedelic air.

So that I fear for you even as I seek
    you out.   Your eyes alone
plead, almost speak to me. "But I
    seek out a plant I need," you say,
"This is the meaning of my greed."

        .

Dear Beast, dear dumb illiterate
Underbeing of Man, where
violence at last comes home riding
the piggish meat, where he will stumble
on all fours, go down, and groan,
enthralld by Circe's wine, toucht
by her wand toward that trans-
substantiation where food, His Body,
    becometh swill, and wine
drags down the spirit to Her will.

Still in that dream I in the depths of
    my sleeping self return to,
I find you wait in the mind my mind
    verges upon. Your eyes
waking from our daily blindness to see
    in that nor day nor night-time light
turnd on in dreams I warily
    remember--   there,

I bring, as if it were myself you need,   the weed
   calld *Moly*.

RITES OF PASSAGE: II

Something is taking place.
Horns thrust upward from the brow.
Hooves beat impatient where feet once were.
My son, youth grows alarming in your face.
Your innocent regard is cruelly charming to me now.
You bristle where my fond hand would stir
to stroke your cheek.   I do not dare.

Irregular meters beat between your heart and mine.
Snuffling the air you take the heat and scan
the lines you take in going as if I were or were not there
and overtake me.
    And where it seems but yesterday I spilld the wine,
you too grow beastly to become a man.

Peace, peace. I've had enough. What can I say
when song's demanded? --I've had my fill of song?
My longing to sing grows full. Time's emptied me.

And where my youth was, now the Sun in you grows hot, your day
is young, my place you take triumphantly. All along
it's been for you, for this lowering of your horns in challenge, She
had her will of me and will not

let my struggling spirit in itself be free.

A SEVENTEENTH CENTURY SUITE IN HOMAGE
TO THE METAPHYSICAL GENIUS IN ENGLISH
POETRY (1590-1690) : BEING IMITATIONS,
DERIVATIONS & VARIATIONS UPON CERTAIN CONCEITS
AND FINDINGS MADE AMONG STRONG LINES

-1-

Love's a great courtesy to be declared,

not everywhere but where the heart's
    a courtier and conceives
its Lord and Lady to be a new Law radiates
    --all Reality its realm-- such
is Love's conceit were your answering love
    but stuff of a passing dream I'd
dissolve my soul in sleeping surfaces
    where transient phantasies may come and go
that somewhere in that multiplicity of
    chance encounters
I might come again to you and find
    Love's court
set up once more to rule my mind.

-2-

Sir Walter Ralegh, What Is Our Life?

    What is our Life? a play of passion,
    Our mirth the musicke of division,
Our mothers wombes the tyring houses be,
Where we are drest for this short Comedy,
Heaven the Judicious sharpe spectator is,
That sits and markes still who doth act amisse,
Our graves that hide us from the searching Sun,
Are like drawne curtaynes when the play is done,
    Thus march we playing to our latest rest,
    Onely we dye in earnest, that's no jest.

[Orlando Gibbons, Madrigals and Mottets, 1612]

*

from SIR WALTER RALEGH'S *WHAT IS OUR LIFE?*

What does this life most seem? but shadows upon
    a moving picture screen,
often untrue to what we would have them be,
    so that we are in our nature
like actors who have not been given their lines,
    or, having their lines, know
not the play they belong to, failing the cues,
    or like musicians asking "What's the score?"
even as the music begins and they must play;

where most inspired, the scenes of a lasting passion
    thrill and then pass on to continuities
in which their promise is undone and lost.
    It is the event of a momentary sequence
that depended upon a place it had in common
    among commonplaces, in the daily routine
of suffering, pleasure, despite and make-shift companions;

our laughter, struck from rapture's incongruities,
    misfortune's rime;
and in the dark, the spectral spectator of all
    expects a tragic loss in what we find and knows
the essential comedy when we fall.
    He judges us but actors of what we are,
faltering in our resolve, resolute in faulty cause,
    heirs of ancient accusations, hidden in our bones
long-plotted designs of our poor demise.

Our persons are but closets that such skeletons reveal
    our species dreads, as in our graves
we lay down the law and return
    the grievous courses of our lives
to swell the sentence after our parts are done.
    In every solitude the common grievance grows.
The grave's a comfort if we come to that.

Our immortality's at best the shadow of a star
    that shines and grimaces and is loved
beyond what we ever were, where we no longer are.

In death alone we are sincere.
We'll not return to take our bows or read reviews.
    There's nor night nor day,
nor reward nor punishment, nor heaven nor hell,
    when all is done and our mortality at last
made evident, we are in earnest and have left the play.

                    -3-

        Go as in a dream
        knowing in every scene deep uproilings
        of earth beneath your feet,
            slumbering a sullen redness grows;

        wounds break open in the crusts above,
        pustulences upon the skin love wears;
            generations of despair   mount up
        into a momentary swelling.   In an instant

        four hundred and thirty-two thousand years
            inertia of conflicting forces
            shows its face raging.

        Against my body, against my soul,
            against my spirit, *I* go then
        into the destruction of the grades of me,
            to the undoing of those hierarchies
        hold
                a vast shuddering underlies
            this mounting of the stairs
        from below,
                        this
            bringing up of the old question

        I will not allow.
                        Old dreams
            denied . the voided images go down

        into the preparations for catastrophe.

Robert Southwell,   The Burning Babe

As I in hoarie Winters night stoode shivering in the snow,
Surpris'd I was with sodaine heate, which made my hart to glow;
And lifting up a fearefull eye, to view what fire was neare,
A pretty Babe all burning bright did in the ayre appeare;
Who scorched with excessive heate, such floods of teares did shed,
As though his floods should quench his flames, which with his teares were bred;
Alas (quoth he) but newly borne, in fierie heates I frie,
Yet none approach to warme their harts or feele my fire, but I;
My faultlesse breast the furnace is, the fuell wounding thornes:
Love is the fire, and sighs the smoake, the ashes, shames and scornes;
The mettall in this furnace wrought, are mens defiled soules:
For which, as now on fire I am to worke them to their good,
So will I melt into a bath, to wash them in my blood.
With this he vanisht out of sight, and swiftly shrunk away,
And straight I called unto minde, that it was Christmasse day.

[St Peter's Complaint with other Poems, April 1595--following his
martyrdom in the Roman Catholic cause by edict of Queen Elizabeth
on February 21st, 1595, at Tyburn, after three years imprisonment
with rack and torture]

*

from ROBERT SOUTHWELL'S *THE BURNING BABE*

The vision of a burning babe I see
doubled in my sight.   The one
alight in that fire of passion that tries the soul
is such a Child as Southwell saw his Christ to be:

This is not a baby on fire but a babe of fire,
flesh burning with its own flame, not toward death
    but alive with flame, suffering its *self*
the heat of the heart the rose was hearth of;

    so there *was* a rose, there was a flame,
    consubstantial with the heart,

long burning me through and through,

long time ago I knew and came
to a knowledge of the bitter core of me,
the clinker soul, the stubborn residue
that needed the fire and refused to burn.

Envy of the living was its name, black jealousy
    of what I loved it was, and
the pain was not living, it was ashes of the wood;
the burning was not living, it was
    without Truth's heat,
a cold of utter Winter that refused the Sun,
an adversary in the body against its youth.

In this I am self possesst of such a hoarie Winter's night
    as Southwell stood in shivering--
a shivering runs me through and through.

O Infant Joy that in Desire burns bright!
Bright Promise that I might in Him burn free!
His faultless breast the furnace,
my inner refusal the thorny fuel!

All the doors of Life's wounds I have long closed in me
break open from His body and pour forth
therefrom fire that is His blood
    relentlessly

"Who scorcht with excessive heat, such
    floods of tears did shed"

--it is no more than an image in Poetry--as though

"his floods should quench his flames,
    which with his tears were bred"   until

tears breeding flames, flames breeding tears,
I am undone from what I am, and in Imagination's alchemy
    the watery Moon and fiery Sun are wed.

    The burning Babe, the Rose,
    the Wedding of the Moon and Sun,
    wherever in the World I read
    such Mysteries come to haunt the Mind,
    the Language of What Is   and I

oo

are one.

-5-

"*A pretty Babe*"--that burning Babe
      the poet Southwell saw--
a scorching, a crying, that made his cold heart glow,
      a fuel of passion in which
the thought of wounds delites the soul.
      He's Art's epiphany of Art new born,
a Christ of Poetry, the burning spirit's show;
He leaves no shadow, where he dances in the air,
      of misery below.

Another Christ, if he be, as we are,
Man, cries out in utter misery;
and every Holy Martyr must have cried
      forsaken in some moment
that from Christ's "Why hast Thou forsaken me?"
      has enterd our Eternity
or else is not true to itself.   But now

      I am looking upon burnd faces
that have known catastrophe incommensurate
      with meaning, beyond hate or loss or
Christian martyrdom, unredeemd.   My heart
      caves into a space it seems
to have long feard.

I cannot imagine, gazing upon photographs
      of these young girls, the mind
transcending what's been done to them.

      From the broild flesh of these heretics,
by napalm monstrously baptised
      in a new name, every delicate and
sensitive curve of lip and eyelid
      blasted away, surviving...
      eyes?   Can this horror be calld their
fate?   Our fate grows a mirroring face
in the accusation beyond accusation
      of such eyes,

a kind of hurt that drives into the root
of understanding,   their very lives
        burnd into us   we live by.

Victor and victim know not what they do
        --the deed exceeding what we would *know*;
the knowledge in the sight of those eyes
        goes deep into the heart's fatalities.
And in our nation's store of crimes   long
        unacknowledged, unrepented,
the sum of abject suffering, of dumb incalculable
        injury increases
the sore of conscience we long avoid.

What can I feel of it?   All hurt
rushes in to illustrate that glare
and fails.   What can I feel of what was done?
All hatred cringes from the sight of it
and would contract into self-loathing
to ease the knowledge of what no man
can compensate.   I think I could bear it.

I cannot think I could bear it.

                    -6-

George Herbert,   Jordan (I)

Who sayes that fictions onely and false hair
Become a verse? Is there in truth no beautie?
Is all good structure in a winding stair?
May no lines passe, except they do their dutie
    Not to a true, but painted chair?

Is it no verse, except enchanted groves
And sudden arbours shadow coarse-spunne lines?
Must purling streams refresh a lovers loves?
Must all be vail'd, while he that reades, divines,
    Catching the sense at two removes?

Shepherds are honest people; let them sing:
Riddle who list, for me, and pull for Prime:

I envie no mans nightingale or spring;
Nor let them punish me with losse of rime,
    Who plainely say, My God, My King.

[George Herbert, The Temple, 1633]

                        *

from GEORGE HERBERT'S *JORDAN (I)*

    Who says that fictions only
become a verse? Is there no actual heart-beat
in which these words arise? no mortal eye
in whose sight the image must prove true?
no immediate life in whose assemblies
Truth in Beauty is verified? May no lines pass
except they do their duty not to the heart's unbroken
melody but to some model lost at sea
    where meaning drowns in undertow
    the mind proposes and mermaids
        raise a storm below?

Is it no verse, no deep imagining, except
the turbulent phantasie pour forth conglomerate
and ominous things exceeding nightmare,
disowning what we would think to see, or speak
as if from the dumb sub-being mass
that refuses to yield to the natural will?
And does a phrase to be of the essential music
we crave demand some craft in serpent-wise word-twistings,
the artist's marquetry, fashiond in cunning,
tail turnd on tail to convey the torque
        that style demands?

Is there no simplicity in what's good? nor in Hell
is judgment satisfied at last but grows complicit
with darker or with dearer meanings still,
disturbance the ultimate rule of the design?
Is there no simple gesture of the hands
in faith to be read as ready in what they are,
and in this shifting syntax no final thing held fast?

Wonder over wonder, wherever the world appears

no longer as a riddle posed but in some
        primary hue,
and men in clasping hands are true.
What's right, no longer sinister; what's left,
without doubt just what it is; every part
true to itself and to the whole contributing
its honest share.   All substantial,
nor good nor evil wavering or intermixt,
no beauty ephemeral or sickening.

I envy no man's nightingale or spring
that may or may not be sacred to the gods,
or hidden spring of some fearful watch he keeps
        where Time's a serpent coild
and the witty tongue speaks with Time's sting;
nor let them punish me with loss of rime:
For I have this simplicity in my God, my King,
that He holds for me the truth of what I am,
        no fiction but a working thing in me.

Whatever I *believe,* my *Art*'s to be true
        to what in truth is my Nature,
            Imagination's Rule, and from
        the plainness of that intent I'd sing.

                    -7-

George Herbert, Jordan (II)

When first my lines of heav'nly joyes made mention,
Such was their lustre, they did so excell,
That I sought out quaint words, and trim invention;
My thoughts began to burnish, sprout, and swell,
Curling with metaphors a plain intention,
Decking the sense, as if it were to sell.

Thousands of notions in my brain did runne,
Off'ring their service, if I were not sped;
I often blotted what I had begunne;
This was not quick enough, and that was dead.
Nothing could seem too rich to clothe the sunne,

Much less those joyes which trample on his head.

As flames do work and winde, when they ascend,
So did I weave my self into the sense.
But while I bustled, I might heare a friend
Whisper, How wide is all this long pretence!
There is in love a sweetnesse readie penn'd:
Copie out onely that, and save expense.

*

from GEORGE HERBERT'S *JORDAN (II)*

As flames do work and wind when they ascend
So do I work my *self* into the sense
    as if the only light there'll be
    is in the fire that tortures the green wood.

While yet I hear a friend who pleads with me--
    Be still. Be still.
    How wide is all this long pretence.
There is in love a sweetness ready pennd.

If we but trust the song I know
    its course is free
and straight and steady goes to work its good;
    it needs but trust unquestioning,
        a burning without smoke,
    a heat transparent in its constancy.

This fire's to be a simple fire
    that would so burn.
I do not suspect its source. My will
    goes with its coursing where it will,
    and every word in every turn
        is so.

    This water is but water. This is
no other water than it is, nor more nor less,
    that's meant to bless,
    and works no magic
        but our bliss.

*

PASSAGES 36   [THESE LINES
COMPOSING THEMSELVES IN MY HEAD AS I AWOKE
EARLY THIS MORNING, IT BEING STILL DARK
December 16, 1971]

> *Let it go. Let it go.*
> *Grief's its proper mode.*
>
> *But O, How deep it's got to reach,*
> *   How high and wide*
> *   it's got to grow,*
> *Before it come to sufficient grief...*

I know but part of it and that but distantly,
a catastrophe in another place, another time,
    the mind addresses
and would erect within itself itself
    as Viet Nam, itself as Bangladesh,
itself exacting revenge and suffering revenge,
    itself the Court and before the Court
where new judges disloyal to the Spirit of the Law
    are brought.   All forces conspire
            to seat them there.

    Terror erodes its own events,
shadows having no more touch in time
            than shadows, yet
    there's no relief from that knowledge.

" Then with the true God, the true Dios,
" came the beginning of cruel tribute,
" the beginning of the betrayal of justice,
" the beginning of strife by trampling,
" the beginning of violence,
" the beginning of no hope."

            Is it to suit the myth yet to come--
the ritual mutilation, the despoiling of nature, of earth,
    of animal species, and mankind among them,
with hatred and, no longer having a feeling of what is done,

without hatred, day after day,
        the burning, the laying waste?

Eat, eat this bread and be thankful
it does not yet run with blood.

    At the mill the wheel no longer turns.
    The fields are in ruin.

Each day the planes go out over the land,
    And revolution works within
to bring to an end in the rage of power
    the works and dreams
of a governing Art.   The air is darkend.

Drink, drink, while there is water.
They move to destroy the sources of feeling.

    When there shall be three signs in a field--
    father, son, and grandson, cut down in their labor.

    The swollen corpses. Flies breed in the marrow.
    Typhus runs in the furrow.

Love, Love, Thy touch is
already regretful.   Thy tenderness

touches upon the angry wound,
proud flesh of what our heritage was

    grown raw.   For a moment,

ephemeral, we keep
alive in the deepening shame of Man,

    this room where we are, this house,
    this garden, this home
        our art would make
    in what is threatend from within.

House made of the changing of the light;
House made of darkness
    in which the stars again
        appear to view;   House
made of appearances, House you

daily bring to me   I remember.

Waking to see your slumbering eyes,
your smile arrived or about to arrive
about your lips, and from that other
     world
from me you sleep in you return,
     Fugitive Aubade I stay by,
How tender the green tip before the leaf
     grows.   Soon all
will be a-flame with spring.

The cut-worm sleeps in his cold.
And in a million eggs, greed grows.
The blood in a billion hearts beats at the locks.
Thought thickens in the veins and swells.
Bright arteries run into the pressures of the dark.
The meat grows restive.

At Xibalba they open the doors again.
It is not the First Year or the Last.
The priests in flayd skins
rip from their cages hearts
to feed the mind of an incoming nightmare.

Who pours into these streams what wastes
     where I come to drink?
What Salmon in this stink grows wise?

     Let it go.   Let it go.

          Grief's its proper mode.

The poem rehearses its lines even as I wake,
     the passage from sleep to day again.

          But O, How deep it's got to reach...

It was about the end of an old friendship,
     the admission of neglect rancoring,
mine of her, hers of what I am,
     and festering flesh was there.

It was very like that coming to know
    my mother was at war with what I was to be;
and in the Courts of Love I raged that year
    in every plea declared arrogant
        and in contempt of Love.

I do not as the years go by grow tolerant
    of what I cannot share and what
refuses me.   There's that in me as fiercely beyond
    the remorse that eats me in its drive
as Evolution is in
    working out the courses of what will last.

In Truth 'tis done.   At last.   I'll not

        repair.

                    -9-

Ben Jonson,   HYMENÆI: or The Solemnities of Masque, and Barriers

    On the next *Night,* whose solemnitie was of Barriers (all mention
of the former being utterly removed and taken away) there appeared,
at the lower end of the *Hall,* a Mist made of delicate perfumes; out
of which (a battaile being sounded under the stage) did seeme to
break forth two *ladies,* the one representing Truth, the other
Opinion; but both so alike attired, as they could by no note be dis-
tinguish'd. The colour of their garments were blue, their socks
white; they were crown'd ... When on a suddaine, a striking light
seem'd to fill all the hall, and out of it an angell or *messenger
of* glory appearing,   thus addrest the Court:

Princes, attend a tale of height, and wonder.
TRUTH *is descended in a second thunder,*
And now will greete you, with judicial state,
To grace the nuptiall *part in this debate;*
And end with reconciled hands these warres.

    Upon her head she weares a crowne of starres,
Through which her orient hayre waves to her wast,
By which beleeving mortalls *hold her fast,*
And in these golden chordes are carried even,

Till with her breath she blowes them up to heaven.
She weares a robe enchas'd with eagles eyes,
To signifie her sight in mysteries;
Upon each shoulder sits a milke-white dove,
And at her feet doe witty serpents move:
Her spacious armes doe reach from East *to* West,
And you may see her heart shine through her brest.
Her right hand holds a sunne *with burning rayes,*
Her left a curious bunch of golden kayes,
With which heaven *gates she locketh, and displayes.*
A cristall mirror hangeth at her brest,
By which mens consciences are search'd, and drest:
On her coach-wheeles hypocrisie *lies rackt;*
And squint-eyd slander, *with* vaine-glory *backt,*
Her bright eyes burne to dust: in which shines fate.
An angell *ushers her triumphant gate,*
Whilst with her fingers fans of starres shee twists,
And with them beates backe Error, *clad in mists.*
Eternall Unitie *behind her shines,*
That fire, *and* water, earth, *and* ayre *combines.*
Her voyce is like a trumpet lowd, and shrill,
Which bids all sounds in earth, *and heav'n be still.*

[This masque in honor of the wedding of the Earl of Essex with Lady
  Frances Howard was performd at Court on 5 January 1606, and printed
  in quarto by Valentine Symmes for Thomas Thorpe early in that year.]

                                *

                    [August 1973]

        Yes, there is a teaching that I know.

Slow, slow, even as time alone erodes the matter,
            I turn and turn upon my life.
Tho I resist the learning, the drive to study it out
                returns.
                          I hold to this and this,
and *this* holds me.
                          And there is freedom in so taking hold

            each time

o o

I hold the matter to be free.

   In the old stories, the protagonist learns
what Time has to do with him.   And in his true
         identity burns within the learning.
   He serves the years.
There comes an overturning of his Age.

   Only *this* time   each time
         in which

               there comes a stage

      a coming to

            time seminal.

There must be another world within this world,
   and a world beyond   surrounding
      this world in turn leads up into,

   a stage of self in coming realized,

      pulse seed of a presiding entity.

   Truth is not mere but in *her* person rides
   and with a fierceness in her nature sides.

   The very thought of her can so alarm,
   my heart stand still and yet so charm

   a depth I feel in me that calls to another depth
   where fear and longing mingle to come true.

      She gathers as a storm a darkness kept   where
   within   a war the outrage of the war starts in us
         answering--

   there being only an intermittent light,
   but flashes of her being there.   In the Masque :

oo

on a suddaine   a striking light   seem'd to fill the hall
an angell appearing   speaks as from an opening in Time:

Princes attend!   Where I appear, an other wonder!
Truth is descended in a thunder, after thunder.
A single flash, her gaze as a constant lightning strikes
heart, all passional centers and radials of delite,
welds in a suspense to attend her will.
So can a woman hold the universe at bay in us
and Time stand still.   She is about to have her say,
she who commands the locks of Night and Day.
Even as the poet labors his verse to find a voice
like to like of an other voice, *impressing and lasting,*
"else the glorie of all these solemnities
 had perish'd like a blaze."   It is a voice
brought to a barrier in marriage as upon perishing
to speak out of the cloud of Jonson's solemn masque
or from that hallucinatory court   Parmenides' Vision knew
in which we are brought, as to a face unmaskt,
to that stage where a woman waits
as if to be Truth.   We grow bewilderd in her smile.
Her visage wavers.   She knows more of us in her play
than we would know.   She shows reproof
that's ever lasting even as her desiring flame
consumes what ever we thought to see in her before.

Upon her head she wears a crown of stars,
"through which her orient hair waves to her waist,"
the noble Jonson would have me say.
Whatever after Ezra Pound would I do with that?
Is she then rosy blond as the pre-light of Day?
Rose Doré in which the painter brings to play
a breath of dawn and truth into his color?
Yet even as these golden chords resound,
I see her in a darker sound.   She wears
a robe enchased with eagles' eyes,
"to signify her sight in Mysteries" --it's but a masque's device,
and yet immediate to the mind's recall,   that's seen
Love that with an eagle's fierceness shone,
rapacious gentleness, that edge
of a fond devouring look.   And doves, milk white, of course,

86

upon each shoulder.   Her breasts are doves
and in the nest of a longing stir.   The image
hovers upon another knowledge of those birds.   The soul
impersonates herself thruout, and an animal panic
starts up the painter renders as the break of day.
The ground she walks upon grows serpent-wise
and with that wisdom writhes wise to a secret we fear,
rose d'oriens come too near, where in the far
we see her greater likeness in the Evening Star begin,
and all of sheltering Night grows dear.
"Her spacious arms do reach from East to West,
 And you may see her heart shine thru her breast."

"Her right hand holds a sun with burning rays"
--O.K. The mode's rhetorical. The manner, grand.
And we've been commanded to put such childish things away.

The river of her being is in flood. It fills her eyes.
Then what's invention or novelty   when *she*
surprises us?   We'd hide our being overcome?
strive for the essential, or make it new?
    She makes her grandstand and revives
emotional enormities, old ways, grand ways, in me.
        Her left hand
holds a curious ring of keys in which rooms
        --heavens and hells--
beyond our hopes and fears   are lockt.

    I'd like to clear the air,
    take on a "modern" stance, Poetics 1924,
    a language without ornament,
    a measure functional thruout,
    nothing fancy, all
    without excess, expressive,
    recalling an archaic mask,
    the gesture stylized, to speak
        from energy alone.

    The essential, nothing more!
    The temper, fire and ice.
    Line, hard cut, without device.
    Eyes, hierarchical, straight forward.

Having that rigor
testimony before the Court demands.

But there she stands! as she is, insistent,
in court dress, elaborately personified,
decorate with *impresæ* and symbolic fuss.
And everywhere, the language is too much.

"Her orient hayre," I read:
"By which beleeving mortalls hold her fast,
"And in those golden chordes are carried even,
"Till with her breath she blowes them up to Heaven."

Now what am I to do with that?   tho I read there is a glow
where men's souls are quickend in her hair and
rise upon her breath toward heaven so, the poet's conceit
turns me back from the myth I know therein.

     There is a Mist
made of delicate perfumes; out of which
     flowering confusion
(a battle being sounded under stage:
 below as above, a war of senses waged)
did seem to break forth in bloom
     from darkness two, ingeminate,
one representing Truth,   the other
     swearing to be true.

The color of their garments, blue. Socks,
     white. Each, crownd. Each,
in all her seeming, to be she.
     Two times in which she
moves--I know not if I saw her so attired--
     I never saw her so.   She
mirrors who she truly is   in
     seeming so. Moving and yet still
she divides and multiplies my sense of her anew.

     I had not known there were so many there.

     It is a magic of a mirroring,
as if you might see her heart shine through her breast,

     a burning glass in which we skry

○ ○

      by which men's consciences are searcht.

    I do not know where I am with her,

and myriad reflections upon her face
lead from old deeps into new deeps of Night.

Princes attend! Eternall Unitie
    behind her shines
that fire, and water, earth, and air,
  contrary tempers in her being, stirs
    and combines.

Nature? My nature I knew not
    in her who held the questioning key
that would unlock in full the answering male Moon,

  furor of shining Man, her Sunne,

      arouse from me.

      -10-

John Norris of Bemerton, Hymne to Darkness

Hail thou most sacred venerable *thing,*
   What Muse is worthy thee to sing?
Thee, from whose pregnant universal *womb*
All things, even Light *thy* Rival, *first did Come.*
What dares he not attempt that sings of thee,
   Thou First *and greatest* Mystery.
Who can the Secrets *of thy essence tell?*
Thou like the light *of God art* inaccessible.

Before Great Love *this* Monument *did raise,*
   This ample Theater *of* Praise.
Before the folding Circles *of the Skie,*
Were tuned *by him who is all* Harmony.
Before the Morning Stars their Hymn *began,*
   Before the Councel *held for* Man.
Before the birth *of either* Time *or* Place,
Thou reign'st unquestioned *Monarch in the* empty *Space.*

Thy native *lot thou didst to* light resign,
    But still half *of the Globe is* thine.
Here with a quiet, *but yet* aweful *hand,*
Like the best *Emperours thou dost command.*
To thee the Stars above *their* brightness *owe,*
    And mortals their repose below.
To thy protection Fear *and* Sorrow *flee,*
And those that weary are of light, *find* rest *in* thee.

Tho Light *and* Glory *be th'Almighty's* Throne,
    Darkness *is his* Pavilion.
From that his radiant Beauty, *but from thee*
He has his Terrour *and his* Majesty.
Thus when he first proclaim'd his Sacred Law
    And would his Rebel *subjects* awe,
Like Princes *on some great* solemnity
H'appear'd in's Robes *of* State, *and* Clad *himself with* thee.

The Blest *above do thy sweet* umbrage *prize,*
    When Cloy'd *with light, they* veil *their eyes.*
The Vision *of the Deity is made*
More sweet and Beatifick *by thy* Shade.
But we poor Tenants *of this Orb below*
    Don't here *thy excellencies know,*
Till Death *our understandings does* improve,
And then our *Wiser* ghosts *thy silent* night-walks *love.*

But thee I now *admire, thee would I chuse*
    For my Religion, *or my* Muse.
'Tis hard to tell whether thy reverend shade
Has more good Votaries *or* Poets *made,*
From thy dark Caves *were* Inspirations *given,*
    And from thick groves *went vows to Heaven.*
Hail then thou Muse's *and* Devotions *Spring,*
'Tis just *we should* adore, *'tis* just *we should thee* sing.

[Poems, 1687]

*

CODA

Yes, darkness.   Out of darkness.

They have fed themselves into their lives.
Wholly, it seemd, they fed their burning into mine.
Dim fires of old loves linger on.
It is the darkness into which they consume themselves
that makes of it all for me a music of no return, of long
    the darkness, the dark fuel feeding forth the flame,
of long lingering flaring up and flaming
    illuminations and dyings down, the ember-life of a
    persistent love;
deep as the darkness that in eyes
        gathers where the light reflects,
in that deep dark the quickening of delite that sparks
        asking looks that change in looking to replies.
Dark as the cloth was woven and the gleam,
the burning chars the weave into a deeper dark.
The residue is ash.

And from the darkest after thought,
still there seems --is it a fondness
        fear would find?--
still there beams a lasting look I find.
I do not shy from it. It reaches
from some confidence you give
beyond my knowing, out of what
dark in you that is all resonance
        fearfully I do not know
yet striking ever true to what is
most dark to me in me from that first
darkend scale of all light Harmony
asking, answering, note upon note of silent
        command of tunings sound
beyond sound.

                O starry Net of Lives
outflung! And our little lives at last
    among them realized!   Elohim-Cloud of bright
expectancies, quickening hunger for worlds
    out of boundless Source seeking its bounds,

the ground of all Immensities, tremendous thruout,
   agony of striving energies thruout, devouring
   Self thruout!   our little household and its
   inner court of our repose found hidden there.

      Nebulae of gathering dreams,

dancing eye upon dancing eye of that scattering of Beings, Stars,
      that casting all their rays beyond
         here to our little eyes reply!

Once in a dream when I was young I dreamd to see into that Well
      of Harmonies, or thru invisibilities,
         the ordinate progressions of a solar instrument
   where planets in folding circles of the sky I saw to sing,
      where seeing was all in what I heard, bell-tones
      beyond the likeness of a bell, soundings of strings
         where there were only ghostly paths and intervals.

      Before the Morning Stars their hymns began,
behind that awakening of chords into Life-Melodies, there were
         darker reaches of a Silence
         to which our symphonies refer.

   Our Father Who Art in Heaven...   I begin
   my prayer before the Night, and, gazing in,
   I wonder at the depth that I call *"Him"*.
   For *Heaven* is not that Spring of Lights
   that burns for Heaven's sake but darkens
         into an emptying of sight.

   The stirring of that Harp of Spheres or vaster
         music of Saints and Stars whirling
   in the ecstatic Rose, unfolding Glory that God knows,
   flows back into a blackness, Ur-ground, In-gathering or...

      Now it comes to me.
   Out, out from the First, from the Void,
      the over-whelming repose of a finality
   overtakes the trembling lives, the sounding
         energies,

and into a Silence I call *Our Father*
        draws them in.

Yes, Darkness.   Out of Darkness.

The joy of an overtaking darkness
informs the troubled vision of my day to come
into whose hallows I bring forth Thy Name.

Give us this day... The house about me
I hear fill in the dark with a familiar hush
into which I will sleep myself.   O gratefully,
I take the gift of my daily life! I...

Now darkness overtakes my thought of dark,
rifts of Our Father blot me out. I'm near
extinguisht.   Return... return...

to ease the bitterness, the wrath
        the toiling path of the inner urgency,
        the burden of our spectral need, the
        debt, the mounting dues,
        to let the protesting furor loose...

There comes not from my prayer but from my blessing near
        reminder of my dear humanity,
you, out of our darkness, have kisst my slumbering eyelid
        and turn from me
"Good Night!"

                How clearer than all prayer, your voice!
    You clothe me round.

        And to the shores
        sleep knows upon a further deep
                solemnity
        into the infancy of a darkening bliss

        Love sets me free.

DANTE ÉTUDES

It is in the social definition of freedom
that we most sense
the presence of the Law:
pluralistic, multiphasic,
liberal, radical.

PREFACE

   Dante "études" rather than "studies" because they are proposed in
poetry as the études of Romantic composers were proposed in music, for
I mean a music not a scholarly dissertation. Dante as Schumann in his
humors might have overheard his meaning. They might be calld sketches,
for they were *drawn* from the Temple Classics translations of Dante's
prose with all the attention to the truth of the moment in reading that
marks the intention of a painter in his sketch books; but in our daily
speech there lingers about the word "sketch" the suggestion of sketchy
impressions, of irresolute work. "Gists", yes, I have meant these
études to come from and to return to create gists of my intentions in
Dante's intentions.

   Studies, in the sense of my reflecting upon my readings and study of
Dante's texts. His is not a mind researcht in the lore of another time,
for me, but immediate, everlastingly immediate, to the presence of the
idea of Poetry. It's here, as presiding presences in a realm of poems,
that I read his *"principium"*, his *"civitas"* and *"monarchia"* to be. Whatever they once were in a world of popes, city states and emperors, they
remain, translated powers, present today in the state of volunteerd
individualities and social consciences and responsibilities, true to my
sense of our good. Each member "princely" in his regard and mine--or
else, democracy lacks rule; each member, a worker for the good of all.
Each member, a source of being thruout. I draw my "own" thought in
reading Dante as from a well-spring.

   But in this moment of writing, in this reading, it is not a later
flow of energies this current enters. What we took to be a stream of
consciousness, we take now to be a light streaming in a new crystal the
mind ever addresses. Dante again enters my thought here--even as I
digress--and I feed upon prime.

94

BOOK ONE

WE WILL ENDEAVOR

[*De Vulgari Eloquentia,* I,I]

           "We will endeavor,
the word aiding us from Heaven,
   to be of service
to the vernacular speech"

    --from "Heaven" these

"draughts of the sweetest honey-milk",

    si dolcemente

from the language we first heard

   endearments   whisperings

      infant song and revery

a world we wanted   to go out into,

   to come to ourselves   into,

   organizations in the sound of them
   verging upon meaning,
                upon "Heaven",
   hermetic talk
   into which my range of understandings
   was to grow   for love of it

      portents

   and adults expounding
     controversial doctrines, personal
     science fictions and
             rules of order,

but our own

"is that which we acquire without
any rule"   for love of it

      "imitating our nurses"

From the beginning, color
and light, my nurse; sounding waves
and air, my nurse; animal presences
my nurse; Night, my nurse .

    out of hunger, instinctual
    craving, thirst for "knowing",

    toward oracular teats.

This,

being primary,
    natural and common,
being "milk",

is *animal*:

    lungs sucking-in the air, having
    heart in it, rhythmic; and,
        moving in measure,
    self-creating in concert

--and therein,

noble.

SECONDARY IS THE GRAMMAR

[*De Vulgari Eloquentia,* I,I]

Secondary is the grammar of
    constructions and uses, syntactic
    manipulations, floor-plans,

spellings and letterings of the word,
    progressions in writing, stanzas,
    conservations and disturbances in meaning

--professional, not noble,
    being learned,
    reflective, particular,

∘ ∘

rereading, instead of memory,
    as if to mediate the immediate,

    needs prayer.

Most of them don't get the hang of it.

Mastering τέχνη comes hereunder,
    artfulness, steady and careful
    (wary) study of the work at hand ("God",

E.P. writes, "the architectural fire,
    pur texnon")

a felt architectonics then of the numinous
    that drives us beyond us, thruout,
    tries us in the sentence, needs of us

"expenditure of much time
    and assiduous study" to read it aright
    as it mounts, the eye watchful

"This syntax is tricky, it gets out of hand"
    the ear taking soundings
    "I have to practice to get it"

--we must come so near, must risk, here, words
    we thought to take as ours the
    threatening currents of ride and so

make our passage that
    the structures of rime extend into
    the fit of the parts at the finger tips

    gathering the thunderhead
    in which Zeus moves the measures.

When the art is one of reading writing,
    there must be a gramarye kept in which
    the old oracular voice returns

to take over the poet's intention
    we cannot fathom, his heart
    in his mouth, tongue's root

°°
in truth sprung.

                    Insufferable
are those masters of grammar
who have denied their illiterate nurses.

Out of dry dugs of their own?

Clonkt lightning!

                    A LITTLE LANGUAGE

I know a little language of my cat, though Dante says
that animals have no need of speech and Nature
abhors the superfluous. My cat is fluent. He
converses when he wants with me.   To speak

is natural. And whales and wolves I've heard
in choral soundings of the sea and air
know harmony and have an eloquence that stirs
my mind and heart--they touch the soul. Here

Dante's religion that would set Man apart
damns the effluence of our life from us
to build therein its powerhouse.

It's in his animal communication Man is
    true, immediate, and
in immediacy, Man is all animal.

His senses quicken in the thick of the symphony,
    old circuits of animal rapture and alarm,
attentions and arousals in which an identity rearrives.
    He hears
particular voices among
    the concert, the slightest
rustle in the undertones,
    rehearsing a nervous aptitude
yet to prove *his*.   He sees the flick
    of significant red within the rushing mass
of ruddy wilderness and catches the glow

          of a green shirt
to delite him in a glowing field of green
     --it *speaks* to him--
and in the arc of the spectrum color
     speaks to color.
The rainbow articulates
     a promise he remembers
he but imitates
     in noises that he makes,

this speech in every sense
     the world surrounding him.

He picks up on the fugitive tang of mace
     amidst the savory mass,
and taste in evolution is an everlasting key.
     There is a pun of scents in what makes sense.

     Myrrh it may have been,
the odor of the announcement that filld the house.

     He wakes from deepest sleep

upon a distant signal   and waits

     as if crouching, springs

     to life.

          TO SPEAK MY MIND

[*De Vulgari Eloquentia,* I,III]

To speak my mind,
unfold the secrets of the heart,
breathe word of it,
take soundings in the passage out--

          even as my hand
writes, thumb and fingers
hold the pen in attention.

My whole life

needs to be here
to come alive in this
consideration.
                        These stars
are fragrant and I follow their scent.
I am their hunting hound,

predator of the marvelous.

I try the qualities of the line,

muttering to sound it,

    divine the ratios, render

        articulate

the actual progress of syllables,

        keep alive

    in the sequence of vowels

l'arc-en-ciel marin of the covenant

        song makes.

                    As if from a flower,
releasing the music that I sense
    a fragrance   a color   in mind

into a moving pivot of the flood
    that comes to me   and promising

        makes sense.

        EVERYTHING SPEAKS TO ME

Everything speaks to me!   In faith
my sight is sound.   I draw from out
    the resounding mountain side
the gist of majesty.   It is at once
    a presentation out of space
awakening a spiritual enormity, and still,

               the sounding of a tone
apart from any commitment to some scale.

               The sea
comes in on rolling surfs
   of an insistent meaning, pounds
the sands relentlessly, demanding
   a hearing.   I overhear
tides of myself all night in it.

               And in the sounds
that lips and tongue
and tunings of the vocal chords
within the chamber of the mouth and throat
   can send upon the air,

I answer.   It is my evocation
   of the sound I'd have
return to me. My world in speech
answers some ultimate need I know,

aroused, pours forth upon the sands
   again and again
lines written for the audience of the sea.

Then what
is "listening"?   The ear

   imitates

another listening in its

   inner labyrinth

   --sound's alembic--

   here,

the equilibrations enter in. Here,
   the "up" and "down" we know,

so that tones are "high" and "low", and

   words have weight in my hand
   as I write.   The argument

       is in the balance,

∘∘
```
there where the tympanum translates
   waves of the air    invisible
          into resounding  visibilities.
```

The shores of the continent

   eroded

listening to the sea.

IN THE WAY OF A QUESTION

[*De Vulgari Eloquentia,* I,IV]

"Whether in the way of a question
or in the way of an answer"

the infant's wail
begins in woe,

sensual murmurs and hummings
at feeding time,

and babblings to the world about
in little streams of joy,

shallows of talk with rills
of laughter running thru.

Yet even then I think I knew
thunderous tides of another kind.

"Therefore since the air is made to undergo such great disturbances
in which God works that it causes the thunder, the lightning flash,
the pouring rain, and scatters snow and hurls down hail, shall it
not be moved to utter certain words renderd distinct by him who has
distinguisht greater things?"

SPEECH DIRECTED

[*De Vulgari Eloquentia*, I,V]

Speech directed

first of all to the Lord Himself

outpouring

"more to be heard than to hear"

      hearing in being heard

[*"...and you, I know from other occasions, are apt
to get caught up in one of your talking jags when
you don't listen to anyone else and it becomes
exhausting to listen to you..."*]

"Still, he wished that man should also speak, in order that, in
the unfolding of so great a gift, he who had freely bestowed it
might glory... that we rejoice in the well-ordered play of our
emotions"

            a Hearing!

  without Paradise

      a talking jag   but

"the place of his first speech
was within."

ENRICHT IN THE INCREMENT

[*De Monarchia*, I,I-III]

Enricht in the increment of associations
I would go abroad
      to speculate
upon the ultimate

"the goal of the entire civilization of the human species"

o o

      not man's domestication, his being
        house-broken,

but civilization, his break-thru
    for the City's sake,
    for the present state of the City,

the first principle and cause of
    the whole thing

      governing thruout his doing,

taking thought of the totality
    in what he is doing...

    a man with a cause!

THE INDIVIDUAL MAN

The individual man
having his nature and truth
       outlined
in relation to groups
appropriate to his household

    his own
    ideogram

    a tuning in

on What Is and seeks harmonies in his
    district
        and in the city

    develops themes
      coordinations
      places and times
      perspectives
      humanities
      public works projects

      a specific civility

o o o
and in the nation
    as, Olson in his *Maximus*:

        to initiate
    an other kind of nation

"for which the eternal God, by
 His Art, which is Nature, [ascribes]
        brings into being
 the human race in its universality"

in   that script   knowing what
    total intention

of which   each
    shown to be unitary.

                OF EMPIRE

[*De Monarchia,* I,II]

Of Empire: "a unique princedom
    extending over all persons in time"

whether it is needful
    for the well-being of the "world",
whether its true authority comes from the "people",
whether and how "God" intends it

The individual man having his own nature and truth
    and appropriate thereto   his household
outlined in relation to groups   he finds
    himself in   freely attending, changing,
    electing, or joining to carry forward
        the idea, the insistent phrase,
        the needed resonance   into action,

seeks to realize harmonies in his district
(his order of life amongst the orders, savoring
    variety, seeking out his space and time,

```
        his life-style)
                                a tuning
    (his appropriateness)

and in the city  develops themes
    coordinations,  names places and times,
    draws perspectives,  advances horizons,
    humanities,  public works,

and in the nation  (thus, Olson in MAXIMUS)
            to initiate
    "another kind of nation"  .

Who are the "people" when "Man" comes into it?

    For "world" read "Earth"

and we know well enough then
    what "sin" and "well-being" are.

        Let the meaning of "nation"

be brought under the orders of the living.




        THE MEANING OF EACH PARTICULAR

The truth of each particular,
    of the local,  belongs to "the goal",
                        is
"of the entire civilization of the human race"
                        beyond us--
how many essential parts of the story we belong to
    we will never know;

    and only in the imagination of the Whole
the immediate percept is
            to be justified-- Imagining
                        this
                pivot of a totality
                        having
            no total thing in us, we so
```

                    live beyond ourselves

                --and in this   unitive.

Thus, Dante makes conception
    primary, and perception
        to be of service, yes,
    but to the vision in which we
        conceive   entireties.

Man's apprehension by means of a
potential intellect   the mode of what he is

becomes so by conceiving itself
    in each individuality   necessary,
(thus the agency of the novelist in establishing truth)
            in the unit   unity concentrated,

but in what that we know?   any total comprehension?

                The sum is beyond us.

"And since that same potentiality cannot all be reduced to actuality
at the same time by one man, or by any of the limited associations
distinguished above,   there must needs be multiplicity in the human
race,   in order for the whole of this potentiality to be actualized
thereby."

        THE WHOLE POTENTIALITY

"that the whole potentiality of
 the first matter
        may always be
        in act",

the speculative intellect
    whose devotions being
    to the general   the good
        of the total design   thereof

        feeling his way

                                                            107

oo

extends into the actual
    as the practical intellect

to practice the good of the whole

the end of which is *doing* and

    making,   enactment

            and poetry,

intending the very
    movement of his hand so

the Creative,   Man

    enters into the Process of *Man*.

THE WORK

[*De Monarchia,* I,IV]

"The work proper to the human race, taken as a whole, is to
keep the whole capacity of the potential intellect constantly
actualized, primarily for speculation, and secondarily (by
extension, and for the sake of the other) for action."

        I enact my being here

        for the sake of

        a speculation in the nature of Man,

            needs time and space (a stage)
            that only peace of mind provides.

Hence: that the human attain
    its proper work, right ratio
    and the equilibrations
    Imagination demands

            to take its spring

            from the hidden

°°

　　　　not yet among us

　　　　　　pivot of what we are doing

　　　　　　sing.

"not riches, not pleasures, not honors, not length of life, not
 health, not strength" --what do we know of from where Life is
 ever moving us?-- "not beauty, but peace"

　　　leisure (time without anxiety for time)

　　　for furor   toward

Justice --not the requital of grievances,
　　not retribution for wrongs, not paying back,

　　but for that   freeing the grievance in us,

　　　　　the fit of the work

　　to the requirement recognized

　　　　　volunteerd   an emotional

　　　　　　distribution:

thus exact riming
and the timing of syllables
that the idea "count"
and custom enter the poem

and that there be heart,

　　　　　a harmony

large enough to account for

　　　　　conflict

in the adequate concept seen to provide

　　　　　contrast

　　the Artist rejoices in.

THE HOUSEHOLD

The household   to provide shelter
and to prepare its members
    to live well   even

in atonality   setting free
    rearrangements of atonement,
daily new keys in dreams,
    reappearances of the "home"
note in the melody.

Let us call each voice, his or hers,
    "He" that leads in the rehearsal,
and "She", the Matrix or Praxis
    the potentiality of Music
            rests in

--it is a choral cantata in the Men's House--

            the spring
of that river from which
        he takes his lead--
each, in this, wife of his intention,
    husband of her welfaring there,

--the women are singing with us   this hymn
            of communal counterpoints--

in the district or stanza, to
    bring each inhabitant   freely
into the action he desires there, to sing
    into action the song, everywhere,
leading from the houses   into the streets and courts,
            a melodious thoroughfare
    "we" direct   in company
        that there be chance encounters
            as far as our neighborhood extends

    we go with what happens--

    "It remains for us only
to dwell upon the mixt rimes

°°
　　　in this matter almost all
to take the fullest licence

　　　...for the sweetness
　　of the whole harmony　　　　　　　[De Vulgari Eloquentia, II,XIII]

　the city designd.

　　　He always wove into his stanza

"one line unaccompanied by a rime
　which he calld a key"

others having their resonance
　in other parts of the city

so that district by district
　in the canzone　reminds us

in the arrangement,　every
　wisht-for licence conceded,

of the familiar places
　　　in the last lines
　most beautifully disposed

as if they fell with a rhyme

　into silence.

　　　　　*

Art may yet claim for itself
in the local　grand exceptions,

as the noble seeks to adventure
　more than is expected,

verging upon equivocation
　the theme returns resolute.

For the mixture of smooth and
rough　in one texture
tragedy　the city needs

gains in brilliancy.

111

LET HIM FIRST DRINK OF THE FOUNTAIN

Let him first drink of the
    Fountain, and then,
adjusting the strings, draw
    directly his measures
keeping the beat of the
        water falling.

"But it is in the exercise of
 the needful caution and
 discernment that the real
 difficulty lies;

    for this (polity)
can never be attaind without
strenuous effort of genius,
constant practice in the art
(of government) (of lines, stanzas)
and the habit of the sciences."

    --the eagle

    soaring to the stars.

AND THO THEY HAVE NO VOWEL

"And tho they have no vowel
belonging to them
still they do not lose
the force of a syllable..."

    LETTING THE BEAT GO

Letting the beat go,
the eagle, we know, does not

soar to the stars, he rides
the boundaries of the air--

but let the "eagle"
soar to the stars! there
where he's "sent"!   The stars
are blazons then of a high glamor
    the mind beholds
--less "real" for that?--
    a circling power.
In holding so he flies, an idea
    increasing exaltation
we know in the idea of it, a tower!

O farflung valiant eagle
    venturing in immensities,
wingd hunger   sent amongst starry
        powers,
seraphic predator!

I'd hover here, a wheel of
    all the real life here below
    swept up--
    the glutted cities, choked streams,
    you think I do not know them all,
    the "facts" of this world, most
        in this mere sweeping-up?

They are the facts from which I fly

        aloft,

beyond our conversation, imperial,

insensate, "high",

    beyond this matter of our speech here,
    into this furthest reach, this

incidence of a rapacious

    silence,

gnostic invader of the "Sky"!

BOOK TWO

A HARD TASK IN TRUTH

[*De Monarchia*, I,I]

A hard task in truth I attempt
Arduum quidem opus aggredior
and beyond my strength
et ultra vires
    so that not by my own power

by no propriety
non tam de propria virtute confidens
(thank you, Jack Clarke, for sending me the Latin)
have I this confidence

    but by the light of that Commander
of all Largess and Liberalities
who giveth in such a flow thruout
and nothing impropriates

    so that in us
    his gift bestirs

    like fluencies.

LOVELY

    Lovely

the way Dante bestows himself
monarchial   throughout   his thought

    and in every imagination

    adhering to his source!

114

THE ONE RULE

[*De Monarchia*, I,II]

        Est ergo

     temporalis Monarchia

the one rule in every   temporal event
    giving realm
quam dicunt 'Imperium'   Dante writes

where we write one imperative 'reality'
    thruout
  one principle one realm
  governs our divagations

       even the irreal

  permeate with that rule, devoted

"a unique princedom
extending over all persons in time"

one process, the coming to the Real,
    the making real,
in and over all things in time,
    this measure
this universe in every thing its reality
    commensurate
this very fount and prime of all right polity

non ad speculationem per prius

    but in the actual

    its ordinations

    to be realized.

OUR ART BUT TO ARTICULATE

  It is in the ordination of the whole

  in each event intent

oo
our art but to articulate

and know the direction of justice

            thru and thru,

"for which the Eternal God, by his art,

             which is Nature,

brings into being the human race

       in its universality"

   in each   just   what he is

         he's yet to come to.

In no thing   final, in everything

         generate of finality.

All that comes into Being, functional.

       When he comes to,

the music of it all abounds most

         fittingly,   its law

in all its sentences is true;

        even man's *miserere*

among the animal variations belongs,

    expands the *Gloria*

         of the plan.

     IN NOTHING SUPERIOR

  In nothing superior

      to his manhood   Dante

--Shakespeare likewise--

oo
            the great poet
nowhere makes us feel inferior
    but there grows in the soul
in reading   space and time
Life writing   in each mind
                teems:
        his mind
ours   a sublime community.

        What's "equality"
to this?
            for each   his own
"whole capacity" aroused
        "constantly actualized"
    self   *in speculationem*
        and by extension
                in actio.

        ENACTED

                Enacted
                in   principle

                    principium

each "princely"   in this
        individual belonging
principle to the play thruout
        the "city" is
            civitas

```
oo
          civil in this
a civilization depending upon each
          one     in time
having his right
          one Poetry
the poem belongs to--
                to what end?
quod est finis
     of the totality  man
          properly belongs to
where his place,  his
     princely behavior
               realized?




          ON OBEDIENCE

[from the Convivio, the First Treatise, VII]

It must be sweet, not bitter
(even the bitter, sweet,
where Love commands
obedience and needs
that increase to all harmonies
the discord    seeking its resolve
restores)
               It must be
completely under command,  not
self-moved (these études,
like Dante's odes,
having their own ease
I feel  and rule  that understanding
```

I've but to follow thru, do
what their evolving likeness will
prove in me, engrosst
in every freedom allowd, draw close)

        and measured,
not out of measure; the words proposed
   to the edge of meaning
and not beyond it, justified,
having their sense so in the sound of it
   demanded of me, I hear
"our" tongue, no other
   I did not know in the bone of me

the marrow music ever I contrived
this "harmony of musical connection"

       rime supplies
                  my own
  true tone   where, reader,

  you and I   must try

the truth that Nature means in me.

ZEALOUS LIBERALITY

[*Convivio,* the First Treatise, VIII,
 "Zealous Liberality" Dante commanded
 his Art to obey]

Giving to all who seek to read,
no word "my own", no secret
language, but our vulgar speech

--American, the word "Principium"!
the Roman Church has let it go.

    Ours, out of Latin,
      "quod est finis".

Having no princely air, no end,

except in each his "life", his
    generous humanity he imagines,
in as much as it takes its likeness
from God's benefactions--
    animal; in every virtue,
cheerful; intending thruout
comeliness in every use,
    "our" good.

And these studies demanded of me
that in my writing every reader
    be *their* friend,
even as I, in writing, *theirs*.

        Finally,
not constraind in action
    but freely given over.

WE CONVIVIAL IN WHAT IS OURS!

O Lovers, I am only one of you!
We, convivial in what is ours!
Out of what fund--your reading,
my giving of "me"? --but this
our zealous liberality. Friends,
in every giving radiant!

O Friend who has turnd away from me,
friend in the turning away,
imprinting memory with the image
    of the gift, of this
turning away   that in my life
    most usefully radiates,
turning my heart and mind from me
    so that I am of two hearts,
two minds, O

Friend who has enduringly loved
what's best in me and tended yet

the rest, of this
giving that in my life most comely
   radiates,
imprinting the memory with the image
   of the gift, restitution
of my self from every loss of me;

O Friend who has distaste of me,
consumed in hatred or envy of what
   I am you know not, this
giving out that radiates, this
   urgency in language in duress
so that I am estranged from me
   to know in each other
what we cannot confess might be,

imprinting the memory with the image
   of the gift,   what else demands

our ever singing out to try again
   your heart in ours?

MR. PHILIP WICKSTEED STUMBLING INTO RIME
IN PROSE IN TRANSLATING DANTE'S *CONVIVIO*

[The First Treatise, VIII, 129-30]

"Why the thing beggd for costs so dear,
 I do not propose to discourse of here."

GO, MY SONGS, EVEN AS YOU CAME TO ME

[after Robert Adamson's opening song in his *Swamp Riddles*:

   Keeping in mind voice-prints that came before you
   again I say to those who have forgotten
   Go

            meaning to recall to us from Ezra Pound's *Lustra*

his "Commission":

> *Go, my songs, to the lonely and the unsatisfied*
> *... Go out and defy opinion,*
> *Go against this vegetable bondage of the blood*

where he affirms his alliance with the spirits of Whitman and
Shelley, and, again, Pound's "Envoi (1919)":

> *Go, dumb-born book,*
> *Tell her that sang me once that song of Lawes:*
> *Hast thou but song*
> *... Then there were cause in thee that should condone*
> *Even my faults that heavy upon me lie...*

breaking the pitch of a modernism for the sake of the beauty
of an outworn PreRaphaelite mode and the enduring love he had
for Rossetti and William Morris]

Go, my songs, then in zealous
    liberality, no longer mine,
but now the friendship of the
    reader's heart and mind
divine; find out,
as if *for,* in every soul
its excellence, as if *from* me
    set free.   "*My*" songs ?

the words were ever ours each thought
his own, and, if he sought
    to find them his,
caught up his meaning in their
    zealous liberality!

Go, songs, even as you came to me,
who had no grace of friendship
from which to sing but
    my love of thee, and truthfully
answerd "I cannot sing" --this
    was long ago, where "I" began.
Friend Song appeard to me and said,
    "However, you shall sing."

It was another English in that day

imprinting memory with the image
    of the command he gave,
a music sang upon the rift in me
    of overhearing.

            "What shall I sing?"

"Make up the song of the beginning
    of made-up beings."   And he

as if moving his hands across taut
    strings of me, commanding keys
he turnd and struck
demands that straind toward
    harmony.

                Go, songs!
Go with all my giving, Gift!
Go as you came in dreams,
Go as you came in poems from an early day,
Go as you came from friends for your sake,
        Go, song,
into the world that's all of song
    commingling!

                            [August 25, 1974]

BOOK THREE

    MY SOUL WAS AS IF FREE

[Étude from the Third Epistle]

My soul was as if free and
    wandering by the streaming Arno

when into that liberty
    descending like a lightning flash
            a woman

123

○ ○

strangely harmonious with my
          condition
    in character and in person

appeard to me, as if my heart
    might burst, and I,
          struck dumb,

the terror of a thunder followd,

violent shaking to the roots
               imperious
whatever free thoughts I had had

    Love laid then hold of
          entirely commanding
all oppositions I had summond,

          banisht
self-mastery, and made in that
art I thought to have in song

          a bond

between my straining soul and her

          apparent majesty.

          NOR DREAM IN YOUR HEARTS

[First Étude from the Fifth Epistle]

Nor dream in your hearts and say
"We have no Lord", for all that heaven circles

is his orchard and his lake;

for when in this verdure
your land is keeping Spring

and in all things that are truly *made*,
    in all true *poetries*,
green springs the mind perceives invisible

        the Things of God,

and in what we know
    what we less know
            none the less moves
toward 's being known,

each event so   just what it is,
    what's *wish*?
In what we'd take as our event
    we prove to be its instrument,
and human wills, where they are free,
    intend and are intended yet

upon Justice beyond justice; freedom

        burns with fires that rage
        from furnaces of necessity.

                FOR THE SEA IS GOD'S

[Second Étude from the Fifth Epistle]

"For the Sea is God's and he made it,
 and his hands
 establisht the dry land"   Then

Melville is right! and Olson
    after him.   It's from the Sea
we've to read what's God's, His
    will and way.   It's from the sea itself
we draw our ideas of the Sea.
    The vastness of the waters we came from

speaks to us.   If it be "God", It works
    in terrible immensities.   Everywhere,

the Sea appears.   Man's
    a walking sea of cells in time extending
            depths and shallows of the form in us;

and in the universe, drifts and streamings

                of the stars,   flarings up of life,   storms
                    out of Time.   Our song

        must lonely and transient rise
            a momentary swirling out
                    or dancing wave upon wave
        from distant impulsations come
                    all individualities;

            out of the loveliness of an oceanic
        slumbering Time and Space waking
            in fits of a persisting fire
                    we ride from unfound currents of
        molten foundations underground,

            here upon this shaking table write,

        here tend our orchard and our lake
            to the Eternal dedicate

        and Art derive upon the margins Light decrees

            in its devouring Energies.

WHERE THE FOX OF THIS STENCH SULKS

[First Étude from the Seventh Epistle]

> "Don't you know, most excellent of princes, and don't you see from your
> watch tower up there where the fox of this stench sulks in safety from
> the hunters? ... her drooling jaws are always polluting the Arno. You
> can taste it in the water you drink. And don't you happen to know?
> this evil plague is named Firenze?"

Out of the instituted authorities and worship of the Presidency, the heart
 of each man in turn grown false in that power, each will in turn
 fattening upon the power, each mind
sick with the swill of long accumulated crimes and mounting pride
    begetting itself upon mounted pride;

out of the side-lesions of Congress:
    the bills and appropriations breeding their trade,

the mounting flow of guns, tanks, planes, fires, poisons, gases,
    fragments of metal tearing flesh from flesh, thermonuclear storings,
    outpourings of terror   even unto Zion

that now swells and bursts asunder,

the remnants of the old Jehovah, Lord of Hosts, of that rule of Jealousy and Wrath
  the Father proclaimd,
    advance, divided against Itself,
    the two identities
        Yaweh and Allah in one   conflagration,
    America's industries feeding the abcess.

She... O where is my beloved Nation?

"She is the sick sheep that infects the flock of her Lord with her contagion..."

out of the people, out of the milling electorate, the millions at work at the
  sick breasts of the Covenant,

the hosts daily consuming their lives at the churning factories of war-goods and
  stacks of commodities,
    feeding their energies into the vast machine of the emptying production,

riding, battling the wave, going under, drownd in the undertow, all, ever,
    gulping at the medium for air, breathing the fumes of the soupt-up tide--

  "She is striving to tear at her mother.
  She turns upon the entrails of her mother.
  She burns for the sickend embrace of her father."

So does she arouse in us   apocalypse

      and in Nature   the Furies stir.

  "Then, though they be unjust deeds,
  Yet are they recognized as

  just penalties."

IN TRUTH DOTH SHE BREATHE OUT POISONOUS FUMES

[Second Étude from the Seventh Epistle]

"In truth she breathes out poisonous fumes"

                    night after night

I turn on the flow,
   the flickering TV picture feed,
to watch the news, the mind's noose
   of violence, starved and assaulted bodies,
   of personality strut and show,
the mounting images of crisis, the
   strain that eats away at the nation.

   Night after night I join

   the millions watching, eating up

juices from the meat at the mind-trough, the murders,
   rapes, conspiracies of evil men,
      the murderous frenzies of the counter-attack.

I know in truth she is deadly,
"...exhaling infection whence the neighboring sheep
   pine even without knowing it"

         ennui
that inhabits violent events
and dresses to kill, sickend will

that stares upon the screen where its disaster spreads

and seeks out the sight of boiling skin

      "infuriate   she doth await
   the noose wherewith to hang herself"

and tires the will toward overwhelming heaviness and

     night.

THEN MANY A ONE SANG

[Third Étude from the Seventh Epistle]

"Then many a one
 anticipating in his joy the wishes of his heart
 sang"
           to see

even in adversity the promised Sun
revive his promise in Earth's daily revolution
     into the washes of the rising sun;
and in the storm, winter come again,
I hear the rain that feeds the roots
     of every flowering spring,
and, echoing, thru darkness underground,
     run streams that will release
throughout the land tears of the impoverisht nation
     from its American confines let loose,
enlarge the rising of the longd-for reign,
     relieve in fullness the dumb pain,
and restore my conscience to its first command.

We have long wept upon this shore
confused and without ceasing have implored
the protection of a righteous king.

     But now the only king I see
sickens in our sickness and every night
ripens to an illness in our need.

Restore my conscience to its first command!
I will return, return to the thought of thee

     to measure wherein I am free.

IN MY YOUTH NOT UNSTAIND

[Étude from the Fourth Treatise of the *Convivio*,
Chapter XXVII]

In my youth, not unstaind
and in much ignoble; in manhood,
struggling to ring true yet
knowing often my defection from
these graces Dante lists
proper to Man: temperance, courage,
love, courtesy,
and loyalty. I speak still
to sustain his meaning in my own.
And, in you, whatever I have known
of grace comes through to me.

Now, upon old age: *"Our life
has a fixt course and a simple path"*
I would not avoid, *"that of our right nature"*
--then Dante adds, himself quoting:
*"and in every part of our life
 place is given for certain things"*:

a memory of the good of things before,
a knowledge of good things present,
and foresight of things yet to be made good--

ennobling song, truth's clarion,
beauty renderd lasting in the mind,
obedience to our common cause
     stirrd once again,
that music that to orders larger than
     mankind
restoreth man.

AND A WISDOM AS SUCH

[Étude from the Fourth Treatise of the *Convivio*,
 Chapters XVII and XXI]

And a wisdom as such, a loosening
of energies and every gain!   For good.
A rushing-in place of "God", if it be!

Open out like a rose
that can no longer keep its center closed
but, practicing for Death, lets go,

let's go, littering the ground
with petals of its rime,

*"and spreads abroad the last perfume
 which has been generated within"*—

sweet warning the heart,
the rose hip, knows
of how soon the rapturous outpouring
speech of self into the silence of the mind
comes home, and, even the core
dispersed, in darkness of the ground
    is gone

out from me, the very last of me,
till I am rid of every rind and seed
into that sweetness,
that final giving over, letting go,
that scattering of every nobleness...

*"the seed of blessedness draws near   de-
 spatcht by God into the welling soul."*

[October 20, 1973]

FOUR SUPPLEMENTARY ÉTUDES

OF MEMORY

*In quella parte del libro della mia
memoria*--
     his *Vita Nuova*
  a memorial.

And in the Mind Poetry feeds
  whose memory banks

before which little could be read

  si trova una rubrica

[and in *De Vulgari Eloquentia*
  he relates the fame of
     trovatores
  he comes from]
       with troubadors

 Incipit Vita Nova.

Christmas 1974 In His Memory

  these findings.

HERS

lo spirito della vita

the X chromosome that comes into
  my conformation

the mother-daughter part of me

(in Jungian schemata the *anima*)

as if She were not entirely
  in my World

o o

whatever inner figure   a
    sum   --and therefrom

    sweet ghostly imprint--

of real womanly presences gatherd,

la quale fu chiamata da molti
Beatrice
            How do I know her
so that

lo quale dimora
nella segretissima camera del cuore

    begins to tremble.

                I TOO TREMBLING

I too trembling
advance into the precincts of
    this idea of her

la gloriosa donna della mia mente

["the offensiveness of his
 mystification of the female principle
 is all too constantly present"]

    the mystery persists,

a depth of her receiving me

    only my youthful urgency dared

the animal brain clearing its
circuits   marvels
    all senses racing therein
round the mere thought of her presence

    imprints

clapping their hands and dancing,

°°
    glancing as they pass

across vast immediacies
        she favors.

    BUT WE, TO WHOM THE WORLD IS

[*De Vulgari Eloquentia,* I,VI]

"But we, to whom the world is
our native country,
   just as the sea is to the fish"

"tho we love our birthplace so dearly
 that for the love we bear her we
 are in exile"

   "and our native speech"

Initially   no promise   we made up

a   truce   a   story

to take our place   from where we were

without   number   there being no series

starting belongs to

a gain in time

does not lead.

Retract in reading again

"again".   To man the advancing line
carries a message of manliness in its stride.

Nor to recover rime

nor to cover   but to   discover   among you

that *you*   all resonance addresses

that *I*   I address   goes⟋ time presses on   [ghost]

the key:

presses on a key   "chances"   designates

"a situation wherein 'even plants have rights'"

"there are kinds of inner & hidden causation"

Passages   I chanced upon   no serious intent

means   the series does not signify

beyond the incident of a numeration

or momentary   alphabet.

"A"   is not "Alpha"   the lead vowel as yet

unnamed--

the message, the intent, the sequence then
we carry

         a kind of inner and hidden causation
exceeding   our naming it.

      Passages "48" names what?
In time?   So definitely "here" there
         I speak from it:
                         the missionaries
meant only to disperse a single statement,

"A Collection of 40 Dances"--not a *series*.

            Name
covers what?
      "yet something fixt outlined the impulse"

mixt numbers
                    he fixt upon
      number words

without   side   number

   It is the count that matters

"We know what beans, leaves, and cows are
 but what does *'eenie deenie'* mean?

                                    [JACKSON MAC LOW]

THE TORN CLOTH

We   reaving
--"re-weaving" I had meant
      to write,
  in twain
     did I want her
to be   entirely   unutterably
   that raging Woman of every "Uprising" ?
     for the Glory   Wrath
  promises in us?
From Outrage
   not denied,   the Denial
     not denied   but kept,
as ever I spin out of kept feeling
   to let loose from my keeping,

from the Snarl
   the frayd edges of the inner Reft,
     the torn heart of our
     "Friendship",   in the rift

   to work now   to draw
     the threads   everywhere tried,
they are like the blisterd
   all but severd   root-nerves
   of my sciatic   trunk-line.

   In pain   where I workt pain
     now I must spin

o o

the twirl of the needle stabbing
    my spindle,

the thread of a contention,
    the only thread my reparation
        may come from.

I may call up a mountain in me
    to sing most like a lark
or wrap myself in the Romance
    of a Dark Lover,

but for this mere

    re-weaving,

for this consent that this wedding-cloth
    of friendship

I had ript apart in what I thought

    righteous

I must draw out of my heart again,

    but without bliss,

    with blisterd and blistering fingers

draw the strands of no magic,

no wool or flax the storehouse of my
    fictions can release easily

        against my being in the right
        against my resolve
        against my undying judgment

I must weave   the reaving

    into the heart of my

wedding clothes;

for I will not let go

    from the years of our rapport

oo
            the momentary
War and the Scars upon the Land
      I saw as
the overflow of our human creativity
      ever meaning
more than we want to know, the debris
      goods and evils
are left, surviving, or to die in starvation,

      lives smoking and stinking

come ever into the reweaving.
The very thread is bitter in its radiance

      draw it out   glistening
into the fabric of intentions
another body my body is

      commands.

SONGS OF AN OTHER

If there were another...

if there were an other
person I am   he would
be heavy as the shadow

in a dying tree.   The light
thickens into water
welling up to liven

whose eyes? who   hides his mother
behind him mirrord in his
bride's gaze when the flame

darkens the music as he plays?
for I am here the Master of a Sonata
meant for the early evening

when in late Spring
the day begins to linger on
and we do not listen to the news

but let the wars and crises go
revering strife in a sound of our own,
a momentary leading of a tone

toward a conflicting possibility and then
fury so slowd down it lapses .
into the sweetening melancholy of

a minor key, hovering toward refrain
it yet refrains from, I come into
the being of this other me,

exquisitely alone, everything   about the voice
has it own solitude the speech
addresses and, still accompanied,

oo

kindled thruout by you, every thought
of bride and groom comes to,
        my other

cannot keep his strangeness separate
there is such a presence of "home"
in every room I come to.

Dread Love   that
    remorseless Aphrodite raises   to drive home   her   offended Pow'r,
I've been your battlefield
where lovely Hate   alone   men call κακαὶ ἔριδες
                        defended me

    contending there ever with   would-be over-powering Adhesion
    severing the Bond   dispelling   the Word
            Eros demands,   keeping the Heart of Things
                at loose ends.

I have tamed the Lion Roar.
It will no longer use me.

Orlando, felix, my little household relative of the Lion,
I will remember to pet you;
    Death takes his time with us.

    Lighting a cigarette. Coming to ourselves.
From long ago   ceremonies of burning and smoking.

    I have burnd the Lion in his own fire.

    The Lioness rages in the hunting field
        far from where we are.

Because of what we love   we are   increasingly at War.
    That Sphere of all Attractions   draws us from what we are--

        In this place
        I make my stand
        and a Line appears
        or I have drawn a Line
        where   resolute
        or in my fear compounded
        I face
        the rapt Sphere
        of a dissolving Pain.

○ ○

    There is no kindness here, no one I would draw into this.

Love that would dissolve all boundaries,
    so that Blake is outraged by the first dissolve of outline
    and rages out at Titian, Rubens, Rembrandt,
        for their in-mixing of light and dark, the color in turmoil,
resolving in him an undying Hatred

that would annihilate all kindness, not
        his kind,
  not like him   I   am   to be
                        --Being Isolate
  even wiving must offend.

        Don't wife me,   you arouse
  that animus the wrathful knight who upholds
the honor of the Lady Anima, her token, that handkerchief
    to be stolen by her handmaiden.   Her confidence

bridles at the touch   in touch   music

  the wedding ground of Harmony   and Discordia

    melody ever upon the point of   leaving   returning
      a turmoil of sound the center and surrounding

  begins:

    Love ever contending with Hate.

    Hate ever contending with Love.

"never, I think, shall infinite Time be emptied of these two"

  "Never", being the name of what is infinite.

  In bright confusion.   White, the interpresence of all colors,
    shining back on us--
Black, taking all back into itself.

    They never cease their continuous exchange.

  The eye imitates *Seeing* particular from particular,

cell from cell,   searches
        for what it's thought to "see"--
this week the track of a monopole   previous to a field of gravity--

   The Sun as if It were an infinite fire, infinitely hot beyond our "heat";
   the Earth turning from summer into cold and dark,
        ice widening over   the sea's reaches.

But in Wrath they are all different.   They dance in differing.
   There is a field of random energies from which we come,
   or in such myriad disorganization   "field" rises as a dream,
        the real   this projection of many dreamers,
daimones, the Greeks named them,   still to be realized   Here

        this demon comes into Being   as a mote

            temporarily   needs

     higher organizations to reveal himself,

        Man so organized   the woman seems taken out of him

            returning to his side   he thinks   admires

--Darwin comments: *"The deity effect of organization"*

                        The two
                        contending Spheres

      (Il combattimento di Tancredi e Clorinda)

                        dazzling,   darkening,

                        come into

                        come in order to

                                each other

        sing

[Nothing in the libretto is for the moment
 not embarrassing --enemies in love?]

      "O tu che porte, correndo si?"

                                Risponde:

144

o o

He--   *"E guerra e morte."*

    Life   is an organization of time to allow
    the suspension of an order out of Order,
    longing then ever to come into order,
    yet prolonging the exchange.

    "It is by avoiding the rapid decay into the
    inert state of equilibrium that an
    organism appears so enigmatic," Schrödinger writes,

    "--so much so, that from the earliest times of human thought
    some special or supernatural force was claimed to be operative
    in the organism,   and in some quarters,
    is still claimed."

                "Guerre e morte avrai"
                                                    disse
--she answers.

        *

Thruout, the Contest, the Music Ground
    where they contend--

Colei di gioia   --forth in enmity--

    transmutossi e rise

        --enter Song's opera

            a smile.

As if in the distance,   arriving or departing,

    the dying or arising of a roar

    --the Arrival or Departure--

            animal laughter

            advancing

        ⁰⁰⁰
                thematic

to all that's gone

                "before".

[PASSAGES: *Homage to the youthful Zukofsky, his looking forward in the 1920s to prove his Art in* A-23]

JAMAIS

must extend beyond the throw of the dice   "a" just now, yet

   no throw of the dice may   chance IT.

      Let us take the excellence of the style to be

            lucidity--

  Clearly, there is no last chance

whether a certain word is to be taken with what precedes or with what follows

   hard to punctuate
   as in Herakleitos: *"Reason being such always*

               men fail to understand"

All ways   men fail to understand.

Lovely, the Dreams and Chance encounters

   but Now   is wedded thruout to   the Intention of a Universe.

     Verse, linkt to the Idea of that Governance,

moves "beyond";

       not for ever on earth   never

        only an interval here entire given a life takes

the octave the first and most   powerful overtone

   given in the Nature of Sound

         which is God's Art, the principle of recognition

--Man's Art, an other   arbitration of the whole

    "Nature of Sound" in which

  the "sameness" of the note   is dismisst.

oooo

In the flicker   shutter/ or shudder   ancient, absent-minded,
    the granite massif   is/ was?   present in Mind

        disrupting the pervasive   overtones of Universe

--so taking place
    in the particular   now
following,   is haunted,   a unique moment   taking over,
    the Demon of Incident   "hugeness"   reorganizes
    the insistent beating of the moth's wings at the screen
            where panic tears apart

    silence   .   the eternal   .   inertia

thunderous outweigh
        "the stability of the central triad"
            in which the impression of a "key"   wavers.

    What!   I do not "know" what I see?
entirely in C,   all feel of "home" abolisht,   Love
            flings itself forward

    at sea   in its work   harmony   dark-wingd
creature of the air

                "the"

AN INTERLUDE OF WINTER LIGHT

              Among the Times of Man
my own Time works in me   turn upon turn
      of an oracular theme   I almost
meet,   almost in this hour
      the dreadful division in the ways,
almost in this place   the sunlight so
      surrounds   your head
is framed in rays   your eyes outshine,
      almost upon your lips   the smile
in which all the youth of Apollo breaks again
      and lingers upon the edge of that
                  forgotten melody
that so sweetly ran on   into my
      trouble with that god   who stands
ever beyond   the mortal threshold   belief allows.

              Fugitive evangel of morning,
I don't know in what sense you are *"mine"*.
      Yet I was waiting.   Were you
barely fitting the shadow of an old desire
      the mind would not let go,   or
do you come as the river of fire in the poem comes
      surpassing what the mind would *know*,
until Life looms over my little life like a mountain,
      the gods themselves coming forward therein
to light the way but for a second *"ours"*.

      The Hours are forever true.   Each
in his season.   In this season
      the flame comes into the agate,
            the moon-swirl into the deep water.
In this hour   as in the first hour
      the honey color flooded into the heart-cords,
            the blood-red veins in the amber.

A second hour, a second time, a second life--

      I do not want to let a second go, and
            talking with you,

o o

I try to sow the seed of what I am thruout,
    as if there were secreted from long ago
        something I was   entirely *yours*
in which "IT" is
    --the purple rose I could not name--

it is the seminal glow of royal dark
    within the sea of light
shown in the visionary stone a flame
    arrested there,   it is...

[*Here the interruption of the poem came.* "What does 'Idumaean' mean?" *the old crone sitting next to me turns to ask, pointing to her program notes. It comes into the poem then, even as I dread it. The initiation has to do with what I cannot name.* "Who is the child of Idumaean Night?" *she asks as if I should know. It's the name* Ida *that comes to me, and I stare into the heart of Mount Ida where the infant Zagreus, Zeus-Child, lay. There is no one there. I've got it wrong.* "It has to do with Mount Ida," *I say.* "I do not know."]

The Ballet Béjart went on to dance the *Pli Selon Pli*
    from Boulez after Mallarmé (Let me get the record straight:
scene after scene is coming into this)
    veiling and unveiling the torso of some
male mystery.

        I am not initiate of the Night
            nor of the approaches of the Day.
        In me   all the reaches of some would-be
            enduring vow   take flight.

[*The password* "Idumaean" *is the French* "Idumée" *in the poem by Mallarmé to which Boulez refers. But now, looking it up in the French dictionary, as if in a dream or fate, bewilderd, I take it to be* "Idoménée, roi de Crète". *Even as I realize I must be wrong again, I know that I have to get into this matter too. Idomeneus* is the second name I do not know to name. I take it to belong to the play of signs. A new person has come into the work.]

    "*Je t'apporte* le Don du poème."

        The statue of Idomeneus

dedicated to Zeus by the sculptor Onatas
        disrobes.   It is a dream from long ago
that leaks thru into my not knowing
    "l'enfant d'une nuit Idumée"
        and then searching for what I must have known
four o'clock in the morning, stumbling
    into whose arms, at whose
escutcheon   bearing the erect cock of the Sun   herald of Dawn,

    so that I know I am not I
but a spirit of the Hour descending
            --Swift Flame--
so that in the place of the cave
    that first came to me as if it answerd --under earth "Ida"--
a second legend of Crete comes forward to lead me on
    where I seek news of him   long gone:

        de semine Deucalionis natus
    --out of Pasiphae   child of Helios--
        Fama volat   Idomenea
        ducem pulsum cesisse
            littora Cretæ deserta

caught by a storm   so the tale goes   headed home   having vowd
    misled by Poseidon   Lord of the Sea's Confusions
to take the first one who came to him   to be sacrificed
            "the one"   he knew not
--such is the Demon of the Psychopathology of Daily Life--
                    came to his
appointed hour.   Some say it was
    because he gave up his only begotten son,   some
because he but promised to do so--
    driven forth from the shores of his country.

[*Swiftly, this foreign matter comes into the emptiness of Idumaean Night,*
name mistaken for name, person in place of person, the child-Zeus, the
father-Idomeneo, the two Minoan princes come forward to fill the blank I
drew for the matter of Edom.]

Who was she, the curious insistent old woman,
    ignorant Muse, or, as in the fairy tale,
        where we must fail utterly to answer,

disguised so to drive me forth out of step
        to fall into step   that there be depth
                no simple thing   but little knowing
I was to be deeply confused

                                --as in a dream

        --the sack of Troy again,

"long ago" again,

        the tempest of Time   Poseidon raises,

        le Don du Poème

                        as it came to Mallarmé

[*So at last the poem returnd to the* Don du Poème *where I found in the notes
to the Pleiade edition Denis Saurat's commentary   which tells us that* Idumée
*is the land of Esau,   Edom,   and that the Kabbala relates that Esau and the
kings of Edom (Zeus, then, and the kings of Crete) were pre-Adamic, presexual,
reproducing themselves without male or female, not being in the image of God.*
"Le poète fait son poème seul, sans femme," *Saurat tells us,*   "comme un roi
d'Idumée, monstrueuse naissance."]

In the dance,   as if broken-wingd,
     a failure,   he   approaches the Father--

the phantom begotten of Idumaean Night.

    Thru the frosted panes, thru the inner glass
        burnt with aromatics and with gold,
    at last   dawn spurts forth upon the angelic lamp.
            Palms!
    Forms of this world emerge within the
        threshold of the light, and,
    if there were rapture, wrestling, the
        advancing figure, the dread conception,
    it has all gone back to the other side,

        it has entirely left
    this relic in the early morning light
        to its father   who remains,
    trying an enemy smile.   The Solitude,

blue and sterile,   emptied of itself,

    shudders.

Dawn Treader! you too?   Lordly
    Expectation of the Day,
are you the one who raises
       these glyphs?

[Thoth *or* Te-ḥuti, *whom I take to be the Genius of this creation in the
realm of the Word, Master of us writing the Heart of the Truth in the
Mouth of "IT"s Risk, comes into the picture.*]

Whom I have seen portrayd, crownd
    in the Sun's disc   underground,
Hermetic, Mercurial, He is
    --Sun Rayd, Christos-- in the Dark
the Shining Forth,   out of the Father's Dismay
    Love's Spark.   What do we know that it means to ignite?
the betraying smile?   the healing agony?

    that you lead us on   to mis-take, to mis-
understand.   Misled we *must* be
    or we would not have brought into the question
the infant in the crèche hidden in Mount Ida,
    we would have forgotten   it was in the heart
the bread was broken;   we would have known better
    than to follow thru the legend of Idomeneo
and the sacrifice again of the heart's treasure,
    the promised surrender of the
first born to the dawn's light;
    and we would never have come along this way
so burdend to Idumée.   It would all
    have been untroubled by that informing
duel of Night   and the betraying blast
    of the Day's light.   There would not have been
pleat upon pleat.   We would never have come   along this way
    to this deserted Minoan shore.

Say that there has never been nor will be   between us
this tale the poem would tell.   No heart
    forever breaks upon this shore lamenting;

no proper king of this country
        has gone into exile;   no father
gave up his child upon this shore.   No tide
        moving up from the depths of me   comes in and recedes
at this Moon's will.   I have no share
        in this devouring of my heart
nor in the swelling music at noon
        of these Titanic dancers.   I know naught
of that father's panic   before his son's calling out to him.

        And of this other romance--Mallarmé's
creative malaise--   I have not truly undergone
        that withdrawal from what Night has given me,
that solitary bringing forth out of words,
        offsprung and outcast poem,
into the judgment of a woman's part in me,
        seeking its hearing and sentence,   yet

I am not unfamiliar with the seepage of the light.   Slowly,
        the drainage of the other realm invades,

as if I were half alive and half

        had yet to find my life.

                                        [December 4 to 22, 1975]

"EIDOLON OF THE AION"

out of Pindar?

*

        Impersonator of a universe
root-voice of first-dream,
     who are you?   Dark Star,
coming back into my life,   arranging
  weddings thruout of
    themes and incidents,
arousals of early morning   --persisting
  night-scenes flow in the day's light.

    I remember,   O I return
       IT
constantly recurring
    transcends its inner organization.

  The fundamental unit of (this) music
not the note but the series as a whole:
      TOTAL
involving every note in a piece

       overrides
  independent of tempo
and does not conform to a regular unit--

  numbers *as such* a higher order of rime

  --heard thru them as thru a grid--

○ ○

as Eidolon of the AION

      you would return

the two halves of the one thought

   close in their   knot, nut, nœud,

as if only in this moment   lovers

   but "making" love   blindly

form the shell to enclose

      --so I *do* know what *IT* is--

   the round of all meetings,   all

         coming together

   in the sweetness of a note growing.

Eros   a little Æon,

   as if we two   were a universe.

The two walnut shells

   carved out now from the heart-wood of the tree

(it is an early seventeenth century emblematic case
    upon a moving hinge)

   open   by their own   (the tree's)   magic

       to disclose

the sweet meat of a little brain   (carved in crystal)

   --Mind   impersonated in whose

     intricate convolutions.

        **

    ζωὸν αἰῶνος εἴδωλον

     who speaks to us in dreams,

° °
you write me

    you found in Pindar,   came to you in dream

(*Here*   for the first time   I am calld

    to work the Greek)   [Nov.9,1974]

                  O Star

    in whose light

        the tree of this rite shines!

Let us entirely die into this long sleeping.

"We met once, many years ago," you remind me.

    I know the time by heart

           persisht

  and yet, in perishing, long left behind,

    remains   "our" life

          thruout   whose Universe

    each comes upon   "sleeping".

Deep in that branching of the Way

    that passes thru the tree   and moves

        green flame upon green flame

    limbs of original longing into dance,

enclosed, all potency, dark-counseld,

    sound   asleep--

    where the intonation of the *melos*

      leads each sounding toward each

         into the sweetness of a clear melody

ooo

    the whole

  time so articulate

lively everywhere   we thought we were.

  Now we return to "our" sleep,   "our"

     time long ago

where   *HE*   shows forth   .

     ***

THE RECITAL OF THE PINDAR [fragment 131(96)]   July 7-8 1979

   Companion, hold steady the beat of the fire that burns me out.

    Yet another body--it is like an everlasting flow of tears, a river I am of, passing, the watery weave of the bond itself and its boundaries-- where was I bound?-- in the fullness of its time remains. The Elohim work their figure of me in the fire storm cloud. There is something in me that terrifies me, something beyond me. In the savage intent he sleeps where I wake, his strength lies entranced where I move and we two would embrace to touch and release our human bond in his bind.

    Deep we go down to die in the beast by the stream where the flow of tears has never ceased we thirst and would perish, the human yearning blossoming up, beautiful bud and full flower, from the stem of remorse- less hunger. Do you not see that my glare would be toucht by your seeing me again? And yet when we sleep, this fierceness returns before us, waking in dream and in the spell of speech the trance of deep poetry his roar the water roaring lion - rose - flame rising round as the flood rises.

THE PRESENCE OF THE DANCE / THE RESOLUTION OF THE MUSIC

He had determined to dance the presence of the dance. He had been in fact determined to dance the presence of the dance, and, taking his stand then, in the determining, he found he took his stand in the presence of the dance.

I am addressing a proposition of moving in a declaration independently of moving. He was about to be moving or he moves into being moving until an absolute stillness became possible. "Now" appeard to him in order to give him time to dance where he was moving.   This lookt at first as if he could return to a place where he just now was. And he stood between simply standing and taking his stand. There was a weight awaiting something. "I can no longer stand it" came into it, and he came up to the edge of it: the dance ground was moving thruout toward and from an "it" he had now to confront.

Here he would have created the freedom not to have to confront "it", had the freedom of the dance not so entirely concernd him. I have fallen in love with the presence of the dance whom now I see then so that before me there will be as ever there is an other dancer.   Where I am he calld "here", and where he is I will call "there". It became possible to change places.

At this stage he made a sign to read THE PRESENCE OF THE DANCE and, waking early in the morning before dawn, he wrote down instructions for the Imagination of the Dance.

"Everywhere thruout I alone will be there," he thought. "Everywhere there will be room meant for an other." This one each time will be calld first a thing happening in the dance, so that in the time of dancing there must be a company of dances to make a life. All in order to perform in its varieties the Presence of the Dance.

"We are entitled to dance *The Presence of the Dance*," he announced.

TWO

There are those in time moving in a great circle so that the figure of circling round comes into time. From time to time, even as the dancers pass around from dancer to dancer so that the circle is circling, lives pass so that the dancers are living. And some-times, as I am moved now by the appearance of the living, Death appears to be dying in the Presence of the Dance.

This is to confess that all the time the Presence of the Dance has been present to me. I was calld into that presence. When I was a child, the world, the skies rolling with clouds, the whispering trees, the opening reaches of a country to be, would call me out of doors, to wandering in search of what was to be out there. Even as this morning calld me to write the Presence of the Dance and the Resolution of the Music for you, and I knew it was for you this very morning was calling me.

My Love, for a moment you present yourself or I present you, and this Presence, this Lord of Title, for he has title to me here, is the Night upon whose reaches this morning calld to me. Oberon, you said, you were to dance. Your role comes into the romance of a play the mind has been following. I said he was the Moon. But how en-tirely my thought ever circled you, taking the radiance of a dark

160

Sun for kindling.

Did I want so to come into the question of an abyss of feeling? The whole company dancing I went round from dancer to dancer as if the Presence of the Dance were every where there beckoning, alluring.   Each place a lure eluding me.   Everywhere lingering, leaving me to wonder. Where I am. Left. Thruout now I am looking for you.

THREE

Glancing passes from eye to eye thruout the company. "As if an amusement had started up from where she had been sleeping. Merle Oberon turns round in the heart of the company where I cannot see him any longer I am entirely missing her in him." The moment calls for the presentation to be unbearably coy. It is when I can no longer follow the star flares.

FOUR

I am trying now to write of my calling, of order, of the order of dancers from left to right thruout the company. The members of the Dance in which I am writing. How lonely this remembering of the Dance is, this remembering of ever being calld. This memory of clouds advancing across the sky calling, this calling up of something startling in me, this about to be happening in the moving from left to right.

At the heart of morning, this memory of a darkness is kindling. Seeds of fire light flickering before the oncoming shadows his eyes his eyes bestow.   Her his grey light eyes cast for me.

Even as I am calld to dance, the fire of the dance devours me.
Unknowing, the Prince of Darkness, my lover, has taken my heart
away into knowing.

FIVE

In the longest night of the Year, awakening to where they are
dancing a Midsummer's Night's dream out of time, a winter's tale
or double take of lovers changing places with lovers in fidelity,
a spectacle of powers to see by and the bewilderment of our poor
hearts at the shortest end of our night watch.   Let me be the Moon
and stand in the shadow of that Wall I see or be it Well *over there*
I saw in whose eyes again I will yet be beyond what I am.   I would
be the Moon crying.   The tears of the Moon flow from me as if I
were bereft of belonging, and so much a creature of the Night that
my longing falls like a shadow before Day into the furnaces of the
Sun.   The flaring-up blinds me.

SO THAT THERE MIGHT BE A MUSIC

1

He is dancing in the change of humors the blackbird fairy prince
of darkness clouded in a cloak of rumorous night he dwindles to
the deep purple shadow under a leaf, Marilyn, the shy girl laddy
we were hiding from afraid to seek and now as in a spotlight of
her drowning finding his own shining reveals herself anew to be
our Merlin we knew long ago in our first reading the story we told.

o o o

It is a question of his music. A questing of music for him. His Muse. Meant for him.

The audience grows restive and they are disrobing. They want to be naked to hear what they are watching. This is the allure of music. They see him as Oberon, le Merle Noir. But he does not want there to be naked people there in the sound he has meant to be pure.

> O Love, how had we forgotten the
> Night Watch, the audience the Presence
> granted us, the Hearing we sought
> in the Courts of this Law.

2

"The title of the next piece is *The Presence of the Dance.*"
"Again?"

"I love the feel of the house lights falling into darkness with only the hearth glow of the orchestra pit and the rise of the instruments tuning. The whole of the music could be in these tunings."
"Those are only noises and sounds, nasals and prenasal wheezings."
"Whistlings, whisperings, whiskings."
"Hush" - "Yes, hushing too." *Coming to after listening.*

"I love the feel of a deep stillness in which there is no waiting to hear."
"O yes, dear, I am still here." - "My mind is wandering."
"Wait for me!" - "I am through out a waiting."
"Listenings, listings."

"What is happening is so truly naked and fully here it floods out taking over from our wanting what we were waiting for. It takes time from us." Keep time in the courses of dancing too.

3

"I thought of the theme as a tree, as the life of a tree flowing out season after season into limbs rounding and a summer's foliage, into green growth anew and the deep bare slumber of old age winter declares. The ring of dancers year upon year surrounding the time of the thematic tree."

"I thought of the melody as the continuation of an Identity in a number of ways" *--coming into the Presence of the Dance.*

"How does id sound now?" - "Again?"

"As I was coming along it was before me."

CIRCULATIONS OF THE SONG
AFTER JALĀL AL-DĪN RŪMĪ

*

If I do not know where He is
   He is in the very place of my not knowing.
If I do not know who He is
   He is the very person of my not knowing.

His is the Shining Forth I know not.
My heart leaps forward past knowing.

**

Would I prune back the overgrowth of yearning?
Free today from the shadows of what has been?
   Cut away the dead Love-wood?

It is as if Christ-rood never perisht.
It is as if the God at Delphi still returnd.

Even now, new shoots are returning toward Shrovetide,
fresh, tender.   In the fullness of summer
   they too will be rampant.
A thousand roots of feeling tamper the ground
   for this abundance, this
         spring water.

Ten thousand leaves of this green
work in the free flow of the sun's light.

*

Do you think I do not know what the curse of
   darkness means? the power in confusion?
Do you think I do not remember
   the tyranny of establisht religions,
the would-be annihilating cloud of lies

        and the despairing solar malevolence
that is rumord to lie back of these?
        the madness of kings?

But now, in thought of Him, the Lord of Night
        stirs with verges of a radiance
that is in truth dark, darkening glances of an obscurity
        Love seeks in love, Eros-Oberon
 whose Palace is Night.   Did I tell you,
        as I meant to, He is all about me?

It is as if Night itself
                meant to cherish me.

                        **

The body of this thought must be a star.

This Mind is that fathomless darkness
        racing out beyond itself,   Time
                pouring beyond time,

in the cast of whose scatterd sparklings,
                seed drift of suns,
I am all water.   I reflect
        passages of what is moving as I catch it,
the shadow of the expanding depth,
the glance fugitive and sparkling
        of but one among a million promises.

                        *

In this world without kings
secretly in every thing   kings are preparing.
See! a single leaf the chance light enhances
        is annointed and   *commands* my regard.
I am in the realm of this attention *subject*.

See! over there as if hidden an other leaf
        in obscurity   as from the depth of its darkness
comes to light   and therein   sets up

rule over my seeing;
all the mass of foliage I see are members now
    of this courting.   I shall derive
where I am   a court   and pay court to this
            courtesy.

                    *

How happy I am in your care, my old companion of the way!
The long awaiting, the sometimes bitter hope,
    have sweetend in these years of the faith you keep.
How completely I said "yes" when it came to me
and continue.   Each morning awakening you set free
    another day for me.   How has your face
aged over these years to keep company with mine?
ever anew as I waken endearing.   Each night
    in the exchange of touch and speech blessing,

prepared thruout for rest.   Is it not
as if He were almost here?   as if we were

            already at rest?

                    **

The rest is an Artesian well, an underground fountain.
The level of the water is so close,
up-welling in every season, rising thru me
the circuit Jalāl al-Dīn Rūmī
in which   at last!   I come to read you, you
    come to be read by me.   Releasing
freshets of feeling anew I come from.

                    *

But if *you* are the lover, how entirely you are *He*.
How entirely He is here; He commands me.

A blazing star in the southern hemisphere

shines in my thought in the north
and I go forth to find rumors of him.

I am like a line cast out
    into a melodic unfolding beyond itself
            a mind hovering ecstatic
above a mouth in which the heart rises
    pouring itself into liquid and fiery speech
for the sake of a rime not yet arrived
    containing again and again resonant arrivals.

Fomalhaut, guardian splendor of the other "sky"!
in reflection my mind is crowded with splendors.

                    **

Are you my soul?   my love?   my redeemer?
O no!   My soul rushes forward to you!
And, in the rushing, is entirely given me anew.

                    *

The veil of speech I meant to be so frail I
    meant to be transparent that the light
    were you to read there would reveal me,
thruout waiting, thruout about to be naked,
    thruout trembling,   has become a net
wrapping you round about in my words
    until I cannot see you.

            Now I would tear speech away.
I want you to find me out
with none of my leads in the way.
I want you to seek my being ready
    in your own way.

                    **

Because He was there where deep drunk I

168

```
      yet rememberd him,
because He was ever in the lure of the moment
      awaiting me,
because His are the eyes of my seeing you,
yours was the mouth of the wish the tongue of my speech sought
that may never actually   have been   yours
was the sweet jet from sleep's loins
      night stirrd to arousal
in the seed of the hour I came upon;
for the glorious tree of that long ago
      acknowledged need
bursts into a like-sweet abundance of leaves,
      as if from utter Being
risings of odors and savorings
      feeding full the inner song in me.



                    **


Have we lived together so long,  the
      confluent streams of each his own life
into one lifetime  "ours"  flowing,
      that I do not yet ever know the first
pang?   the confused joyous rush
      of coming to myself in you?
            the leap at the brink of being
left alone?   the solitary on-going
      before you?   I am ever before you,
even in the habit of our sweet marriage
      of minds.   Yet I am not
            so sure of finding you
that I have no need for this
      reassurance,
for the embrace of our two bodies,
      for the entwining of bodies,
for the kiss,  even as the first kiss,

for the memorial seal into silence the
      lips bound,
the joyous imprint and signature of our
      being together   one
```

in the immortal ellipse.

                     *

For how entirely mortal is the love I bear for you.
I bring it forward into the full fragrant
      flare, the rosy effulgence   of a perishing tree.

As in Oz or in fairyland, the fruits of that
      arbor   are ever changing.
All the flowering specters of my   childhood and manhood
      come into and fade into   that presence,
perilous thruout, essential thruout
      --apple, cherry, plum--deep purple
      as night and as sweet--quince and pear--
we know they are all there   all ready,
      in each ring, each year
they belong to the tree's inner preparing.

For how entirely a door has been flung open in me
                  long prepared!
How each season of the year, a thief,
      goes in and goes out,
bearing transgressions of tastes and odors,
      traces of me lost,
imprints of thee, stolen hours,
      stored among my secrets.

                  **

Stand by me!   you wingd and
            dark ascendant!
Attend me!   Here!   Falling!

                  *

For I am falling out into that Nature of Me
      that includes the Cosmos it believes in

as if it were the smallest thing, an all but invisible
    seed in the cloud of these seeds scatterd,
ever emerging from belief   beyond belief.

I shall never return into my Self;
    that "Self" passes out of Eternity, incidental!

He too seeks you out. He too
    dreams of coming to this fugitive morning,
of finding His "Self" in a Time so personal
    it is lost in our coming into it.

                        *

Again you have instructed me to let go,
to hold to this falling, this
    letting myself go.
I will succumb entirely to your intention.

        Contend with me!
    you demand. And I am surrounded by wingd
        confusions. *He*
is everywhere,   nowhere
    now where I am.

In every irreality there is Promise.
    But there
where I am not   *He*   really is.

    In Whose Presence
it is as if I had a new name.

                    **

I am falling into an emptiness of Me,
every horizon   a brink of this emptying,
walls of who-I-am falling into me.

How enormous to come into this need!
Let us not speak then of full filling.

○ ○

In the wide Universe
    emptying Itself into me, thru me,
in the myriad of lights falling,

let us speak of the little area of light
    this lamp casts.
Let us speak of what love there is.
Let us speak of how these perishing
    things
uphold me   so that

    I fall

        into *Place*.

                    *

The child I was has been left behind.
Those who first loved me have gone on without me.
Where they were   a door has been left open   upon a solitude.
In the midst of our revelry I find myself waiting.

Every day the sun returns to this place.
Time here advances toward another summer.
These fruits again darken;   these new grapes
will be black and heavy hang from their bough.   The heat at noon deepens.

Sweet and pungent each moment ripens.
Every day the sun passes over this valley.
Lengthening shadows surround me.
All day I waited.   I let the sun and shadow pass over me.

Here a last clearing of sunlight is left amidst shadows.
The darkest shadow falls from my pen as it writes.
In this farewell the sun pours over me
hot as noon at five o'clock.

But in Rūmī's text it is dawn. At last
    he will come for me!
He has climbed over the horizon like the sun," I read.

Where have you gone?
"He is extinguishing the candles of the stars."

Come quickly here where the sun is leaving me, Beloved,
for it is time to light the lovely candles again!

**

For a moment did Beauty pass over my face?
I did not have to reach for *your* beauty.
Radiant, it entirely flowd out and thru me.

Were you talking?   Were we discoursing
    upon the mercurial Hermes?

The mysteries of quick-silver and the
    alchemical gold,
the transports of Beauty,   dissolve themselves
    and are nothing,
--are resolved again,   everything--
    a wave of my own seeing you
in the rapture of this reading.

    What were you saying?
An arrow from the shining covert of your gaze
    pierced me.   Molten informations of gold
flood into my heart, arteries and veins,
    my blood,   racing thruout with this news,
pulses in a thousand chemical
    new centers of this learning.

*

How long ago I would have been your target!
every line of my young body alert to be drawn into your sight!
All of my youth was meant to be your target.

Now so late that my body
darkens and the gossip of years
goes on loosening the tides of

my body,   now so late that
the time of waiting itself loosens
new pains in me, I hear
the sound of the bow-string.

    Swift, swift, how again
and again that arrow   reaches me

    and fails to reach me!

                    **

How I long for the presence of your eyes,
for in your eyes gnostic revelations
    come to me,   Hermes
darkens and quickens my speech.

I will take up geometry again.
The mysteries of here and there,   above and below,
    now and then, demand new
figures of me.   A serpent intuition
    flickers its tongue upon the air.

Mine now the quickening of that
    shifting definition I am swaying in whose

    fascination suspended   before striking

which now opens out radiant and singing petals from itself
    so that I am lost in its apparition,
distracted in this looking into the time-sway.

I am like a snake rising in the
    mirage of the sun where
everything is swaying,   to and fro,
    noon visual dancing and,
beyond my hearing, in seeing I over-hear
    the messengers of the sun buzzing,   wingd.

I see and am held here in my seeing before striking
    the honeyd glow of the woodwind dance

            singing.

In each House   He has a different name.
In each   He is expected again.

And I too change, but you in all
    these years remain
true to me so that it most seems,
        sweet constancy
    in you I have come true
and all the rest is range.

Then *He* is range.   And from this household ours
    Heaven is range.   In the Grand Assemblage of Lives,
        the Great Assembly-House,
this Identity, this Ever-Presence,   arranged
    rank for rank, person for person, each from its own
sent out from what we were   to another place
    now in the constant exchange

        renderd true.

**